SELL Your HOME in ANY MARKET

50
Surprisingly Simple Strategies for Getting Top Dollar Fast

JIM REMLEY, ABR, ALHS

ᴬMACOM

American Management Association

New York • Atlanta • Brussels • Chicago • Mexico City • San Francisco
Shanghai • Tokyo • Toronto • Washington, D.C.

Special discounts on bulk quantities of AMACOM books are available to corporations, professional associations, and other organizations. For details, contact Special Sales Department, AMACOM, a division of American Management Association, 1601 Broadway, New York, NY 10019.
Tel.: 212-903-8316.   Fax: 212-903-8083.
Web Site: www.amacombooks.org

This publication is designed to provide accurate and authoritative information in regard to the subject matter covered. It is sold with the understanding that the publisher is not engaged in rendering legal, accounting, or other professional service. If legal advice or other expert assistance is required, the services of a competent professional person should be sought.

Library of Congress Cataloging-in-Publication Data

Remley, Jim, 1969–
  Sell your home in any market : 50 surprisingly simple strategies for getting top dollar fast / Jim Remley.
       p.   cm.
    Includes index.
    ISBN-13: 978-0-8144-0028-9
    ISBN-10: 0-8144-0028-0
    1. House selling.   2. Real estate business.   3. Real property.   I. Title.

  HD1379.R46 2008
  643'.12—dc22

                                                      2007043681

REALTOR® is a registered collective membership mark that identifies a real estate professional who is a member of the NATIONAL ASSOCIATION OF REALTORS® and subscribes to its strict code of ethics.

Printing number

10   9   8   7   6   5   4   3   2

Contents

Introduction

Congratulations! You have decided to sell your home. But it's a little scary, right?

Don't worry, you're not alone. Selling a home is a life-changing event, and no matter how expensive or inexpensive your home might be, to you, the homeowner, it's a huge financial decision. It doesn't matter whether you own a cottage in a small town or a luxury apartment in Chicago; when it comes time to sell, every seller wants to find a buyer who is ready, willing, and able to purchase his home at a fair price and on fair terms.

Of course, from the outside looking in, selling a home can seem pretty straightforward: Just put a sign in the lawn, throw a few ads in the local paper, and bingo, there should be a line of potential buyers lined up down the street, right? Well, probably not. The truth is, in today's hypercompetitive and Internet-enabled real estate market, buyers have access to hundreds or even thousands of homes to preview prior to making a purchase. For a seller, this means that you will have to compete for a buyer's attention, and today the competition is fierce.

The good news is that every home has a buyer. Yes, the person who will eventually purchase your home is alive and well and is today walking the earth just waiting for the opportunity to write an offer on your home. The challenge is to position your home in such a way that this particular buyer finds it and, more importantly, finds it attractive enough to actually complete a purchase. This is important because as a seller, you probably have three distinct goals. First, you want to sell your home for the largest amount of money possible;

second, you want to sell within your own time frame; and finally, you want the least amount of hassles possible. This book is designed to provide you with the best information, strategies, and techniques for achieving all of these goals regardless of the market conditions. Good or bad, up or down, buyer's market or seller's market, you can sell your home!

Now you might ask: "How can you say that with confidence? After all, you've never even seen my home." As a real estate professional for the last 18 years and the owner of 11 real estate offices, I've discovered that successful sellers, the ones who sell their homes 100 percent of the time despite the market conditions, have leveraged their ability to sell by using powerful tools that are available to anyone. Contained in these pages are more than 50 of these time-tested techniques that you can begin using to get your home sold today.

So are you ready to find out how to sell your home in any market? Let's get started.

C H A P T E R   1

The Big Decision: Is This the Right Time to Sell Your Home?

As you think back over your life, you can probably remember all of the homes that you or your parents have lived in. If you're like me, you might even remember the rooms—the places where you slept, ate, fought, played, and laughed. A home is a special place. It's more than just four walls and a roof; a home, your home, is a reflection of where you are in your life. It's a reflection of your lifestyle.

This may be one reason why today nearly 70 percent of American families own a home, more than at any other time in the nation's history. What's more, according to the most recent data from the National Association of REALTORs, on average these same families will sell their current home and buy a new one in the next two to six years. Imagine that: The entire country will be selling their homes and buying new ones in the next 24 to 72 months.

Why so often? For first-time homeowners, a first home, like a first car, is a temporary stop on the way to bigger and better things. The cute cottage that was once cozy, even romantic with a blushing bride, can now seem cramped with two kids climbing the walls and a retriever doing laps down the hall. Then there's the fact that as we become more successful, what we want in our home often grows with us, changing and adapting to our needs. A home office, a family room, a formal dining room, or a master bedroom suite—they're all just stops on the road to living the American Dream. Likewise, as life "happens," we may have a sudden need to downsize because of the loss of a job or a medical emergency, or a move may be necessary because of a job transfer, or because we need to cash in our chips because of a divorce.

Table 1-1 gives the most common reasons for selling.

TABLE 1-1
PRIMARY REASON FOR MAKING A HOUSING CHANGE

Home is too small	19%
Neighborhood has become less desirable	13%
Change in family situation	11%
Move closer to job	10%
Move closer to friends and family	9%
Job relocation	9%
Home is too large	7%
Retirement	5%

From National Association of REALTORs, *2006 Profile of Home Buyers and Sellers.*

There is a psychology to selling that many sellers experience but rarely take the time to analyze. It is the process of moving from being completely satisfied, happy, and content in their present home to being dissatisfied, unhappy, and downright miserable. It doesn't happen overnight, but it does happen relatively quickly, as most of us will move on to our next casa before the warranty runs out on the new Honda parked in our driveway.

So how does this process take place? Often it starts with a homeowner beginning to notice other, more desirable castles. This could be a friend's condo that has an extra bathroom or a home theater room, or maybe it's a ranchette that you notice on the way to work that has a covered porch and a picturesque view of a valley. For others, it might be as simple as picking up a real estate guide and flipping through the pages while daydreaming about how nice it would be to get out of the city. From there, it's easy for homeowners to find themselves searching the Internet, attending open houses, talking to a REALTOR, or even randomly driving through neighborhoods in search of their next address.

Yes, it's interesting; almost all sellers first arrive at the doorstep of the real estate market as buyers in disguise, and while it may take months to roll this decision up a mountain of doubt, anxiety, and concern, as soon as we begin to see homes that better reflect our current lifestyle, many of us will decide that we can hardly wait to purchase our next home.

Of course, unless you have won the lottery, have a trust fund, or made it big in pork bellies, in order to buy your next dream home, you will first have to sell your current residence. So hold on to your hat. It's time to park the car, put down the mouse, and close the magazine. Why? It's time to get to work selling your home!

Finding Your Pain

Here is a weird but absolutely true fact: The reason you are even considering selling is because continuing to live in your current home is too painful for you. Now when I say painful, I don't mean that you go home crying every night or that something is physically hurting you, but that there is something that bothers you about your current residence. In the real estate business, we call this finding a client's pain, or what it is about your current abode that sticks in your craw enough to make you consider a move. This pain can range from extremely mild, bordering on nonexistent, to extremely irritating, and in some cases lifestyle threatening.

You see, there are really two kinds of sellers in the world: the necessary seller and the optional seller (see Figure 1-1). The necessary seller has no choice but to move; it's a forced sale. For instance, the seller may have been transferred, or he may be going through a divorce, or perhaps he is entering bankruptcy. So selling is a given; it's something that he has

Figure 1-1

Necessary Seller
High Need to Sell

MOTIVATION

Optional Seller
Low Need to Sell

to do because he has no choice. For these sellers, their pain level is very high; in other words, if they don't sell, bad things are going to happen. They could lose their job, they could end up living with their ex-husband or ex-wife, or they could lose their credit rating.

On the other end of the spectrum is the optional seller. The optional seller is a homeowner who has made the decision to sell because she is ready for a lifestyle change. For one reason or another, she is unhappy with her current residence. This may mean that she wants to move to a new school district, she wants to live in a more modern home, or perhaps she just wants a larger space to entertain her friends and family. She doesn't have to sell; she just wants to sell. Of course, this doesn't mean that these homeowners can't be highly motivated. Often an optional seller can be so unhappy with her current living arrangements that her level of pain is extremely high. And yet, unlike the necessary seller, if for some reason she can't sell her home, nothing bad will happen, other than being frustrated, irritated, and perhaps more than a little depressed. Her world won't come crashing down.

So can you see the difference? Good, because most sellers don't understand their own motivation level. I'll give you a classic example: We'll call this couple Jeff and Sally HardNose.

> **Jeff and Sally HardNose are excited. They just got the news that Sally has been offered a huge promotion that will nearly double her pay. The only downside is that the job is in another city, which means that they will have to sell their beloved condo. Despite this, Sally accepts the new job and agrees to move immediately while Jeff stays behind to sell the condo.**

So what kind of sellers are Jeff and Sally? Are they best described as necessary sellers or as optional sellers? Easy question, right? They are definitely necessary sellers; their pain level is high. They need to sell quickly. But do they know that?

> **Jeff does some research. He discovers that condos in their building are selling for between $300,000 and $320,000, depending on the particular unit's**

amenity package. After thinking about it for a couple of days, Jeff and Sally decide to begin marketing the condo at a price of $350,000. Their reasoning is that they can always come down, but they can't go up, so it's probably best to start high.

After a month of advertising, they have received only five phone calls, four from REALTORs who wanted to show the home to prospective buyers, and one from a buyer who hung up after hearing the price. Jeff decides not to work with the buyers represented by the real estate agents, since Sally is against paying a commission. So they wait.

As another month passes, Jeff and Sally begin to fight over the house. They are now paying for two households—two rents, two sets of utility bills, two of everything. The financial strain is taking a toll on their marriage. Still they hold out for $350,000.

After two more long months with no offers and only three showings, they cut the price to $300,000 and make the hard decision to list the home with a real estate professional. Within 30 days the home sells and Jeff and Sally end up netting $288,000 after closing.

Jeff and Sally fell into a classic trap. They did not understand their own motivation level. If they had accepted the fact that they were really necessary sellers who had to sell quickly, they might have made drastically different decisions that could have saved them tens of thousands of dollars.

What different decisions might they have made? Here are three key decisions they could have made that might have changed their outcome dramatically:

- *Price the property to the market.* If they had priced the property more accurately, perhaps between $300,000 and $320,000, they would have been more competitive with the other condos in their building.

- *Offer incentives to prospective buyers.* They could have offered incentives to buyers, like help with closing costs or an interest-rate buy-down. (More on this strategy later.)
- *Cooperate with real estate professionals.* They could also have hired a real estate professional earlier, or at the very least cooperated with those agents who had called with a prospective buyer in mind.

So here is an interesting question: Do you understand your own level of pain? Let's find out just how motivated you are by doing a quick exercise. Write down your three biggest reasons for selling your home.

My three biggest reasons for selling my home now are:

1. _____

2. _____

3. _____

Next, on a scale of 1 to 10, with 1 meaning that you love your home and never want to leave it and 10 meaning that you need to sell your home today, rate your level of motivation:

My motivation level is a _____.

How motivated you are as a seller will influence nearly every decision you make when it comes to successfully marketing your home. But here's an interesting question: What if you and your significant other have different levels of motivation? Believe it or not, this is a common dilemma because often one person in a family wants to sell more than the other person. Why? His level of pain is higher.

The best way out of this bind is to decide as a couple what your true level of motivation is and commit to a plan of action that achieves your family housing goals. This may involve an intense debate, a friendly discussion, or just an extra round of margaritas at your local watering hole. Regardless of how you get there, once you know as a couple why you are selling and how motivated you are to sell, you will have a key advantage over most sellers in the marketplace. You will know exactly how important it is for you to move and, more importantly, how far you are willing to push the envelope to actually get the home sold.

STRATEGY 1

Determine your motivation level.

This is critical because, as every successful seller knows, it's not a question of whether you can sell your home, but a question of when and for how much! This is one reason why it's so important to understand the market.

Five Ways to Understand and Review the Real Estate Market

So what the heck is "the real estate market," anyway? We hear about it all the time in the newspaper, on television, and even online. But what does it mean?

For economists, the real estate market is often best described as the demand for housing at any given point in time. This snapshot is then used to compare the current market conditions to those at an earlier point in time to determine a trend line. For instance, as seen in Figure 1-2, if sales have increased compared to a year ago, then the market might be said to be "up"; on the other hand, if closings have fallen, the market might be said to be "down."

Figure 1-2

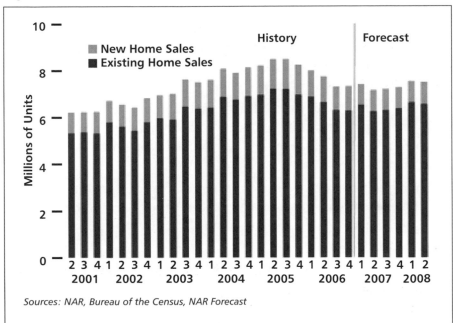

Sources: NAR, Bureau of the Census, NAR Forecast

Simple enough, right? Well, that's only one way to measure the market. The market can also be measured using several other different metrics, including the average days on market, the average sales price, or even the average difference between list and sales price, to name just a few. This wide array of possible measurements is why if you talk to 10 different people and ask them to describe your local real estate market, you might get 10 different answers. Unlike the stock market, the bond market, or even the commodities market, the real estate market cannot be defined by large barometers or indexes. This is one reason why you can't watch the CNN news ticker and say, "Oh, honey, look; the real estate market lost 100 points today."

STRATEGY 2

Clearly understand the local real estate market.

To gauge your own market accurately, it might be wise to take the counsel of the British physician Dr. Thomas Fuller, who famously said, "Get the facts, or the facts will get you. And when you get 'em, get 'em right, or they will get you wrong." That's good advice. So how can you determine what kind of market you have in your own area? Let's take a look at five key numbers you must know before placing your home on the market.

Five Key Market Numbers:

1. *Average sale price.* This figure represents the combined sale prices for all of the homes sold in your local market divided by the total number of sales.

2. *Average listing price.* In contrast to what people actually sell their homes for, this number indicates the average price that home-owners are asking for when they initially begin to market their homes.

3. *Average difference between list price and sale price.* This number (usually expressed as a percentage) indicates the average difference between what people list their homes for and what they eventually sell their homes for.

4. *Average days on market.* This is the length of time that it takes the average seller from the time she begins marketing her home to the date of closing.

5. *The inventory on hand.* This number (generally expressed in months, weeks, or days) represents how long it would take to exhaust the current inventory based on the current selling rate if no more homes were listed.

To put these numbers to work, let's dissect where the market seems to be trending for a fictional city and see how this might affect a potential seller (see Figure 1-3).

Figure 1-3

OVERALL MARKET CONDITION REPORT

	July 2005	July 2006	%
Listings:			
New #	122	135	+10.6%
Total #	1321	1421	+7.5%
Sales:			
Pending #	154	132	−14.2%
Closed #	111	109	−1.8%
Average LP	$394,400	$421,000	+6.8%
Average SP	$392,000	$412,500	+5.2%
LP vs. SP	99.5%	98%	−1.5%
DOM	28 Days	39 Days	+39%

Let's start our review with the average sales price, which in this market has gone up 5.2 percent in the last year. This is good news for buyers and sellers. It means that homeowners are seeing strong appreciation on their housing investments.

Next, take a look at the average listing price. Sellers appear to be bullish about the market. Not only have they increased their asking prices by an average of 6.8 percent in the last 12 months, but they are also holding out for top dollar by dropping their price an average of only 1.5 percent when they receive an offer. The future seems bright. But could there be problems on the horizon?

Unfortunately, the answer is yes. To find the potential problem, let's dig deeper and look at the average days on market. Remember, the average days on market is how long it takes a seller from start to finish to get his home sold. In this market, this key indicator has jumped from 28 days to 39 days, a nearly 40 percent increase in the length of time it takes to get a home sold. I know you might be thinking: "Hey, 39 days doesn't seem like a long time." The trouble is, if this is part of an overall trend, it could be pointing to a bigger problem.

To find out, let's look at the last piece of data in our list of key numbers: the inventory sell-off rate. We can determine this figure by simply dividing the total number of listings on the market today by the number of closed sales for the previous month. In this case, that means that we divide 1,421 listings by 109 sales. When we do this, we get a whopping 13.04 months of inventory. This is a huge number! It means that if no more listings were taken in this market, it would take more than 13 months just to sell off the current inventory.

So what do you make of all these numbers? Do they seem to indicate a buyer's market or a seller's market? To answer this question, let's quickly define the difference between the two.

Defining Your Market: Buyer's Market vs. Seller's Market

Buyer's market. A real estate environment that is advantageous to buyers. This can often mean that buyers are benefiting from:

- A large inventory of homes to choose from
- Stable or slow growth in housing prices
- Motivated sellers and more forced sales
- Incentives offered by sellers and builders

Seller's market. A real estate environment that is advantageous to sellers. This can often mean that sellers are benefiting from:

- A small or shrinking inventory of homes to choose from
- Strong appreciation rates
- Pricing power—sellers are holding out for top dollar
- Multiple offers and bidding wars

Of course these two types of markets, a buyer's market and a seller's market, are the ones we hear about most, but believe it or not, there's actually a third alternative—a transitional market. Yes, just like in your high school science class, where you learned that a compound can exist as a solid, a liquid, or a gas, the real estate market can move from a buyer's market, to a transitional market, to a seller's market and then back again.

So what is this mysterious transitional market state? Let's take a quick look.

The Third Alternative: A Transitional Market

Transitional market. A market that is in a fluid state; it can easily heat up and turn into a seller's market or just as easily cool off and become a buyer's market, depending on market forces. Often in a transitional market:

- The market numbers will be mixed, with no clear winners.
- It may take several weeks or months to see a tipping point.
- Buyers and sellers both believe they are in control.
- Buyers and sellers resist the move away from their market.
- There may be pockets of strong growth and pockets of stagnation.

So let's go back to our earlier fictional market overview. Remember, this is a market environment that is full of mixed signals—strong appreciation, but a huge inventory; strong listing to sale price percentages, but increasing market times. What should this indicate to us as smart home sellers? Yes, this is clearly a market in transition, a market that is at the moment fluid but could easily tip into a buyer's market or just as easily seesaw back into a hot and heavy seller's market.

Now I'll make a wager with you. I'll bet you that almost no one in this market actually knows what's happening. It's true. But for you the successful home seller, knowledge is power. The more knowledgeable you are about the real estate market, the more likely you are to be able to position your home so that it will successfully sell for top dollar, in your time frame, and with the least amount of hassles regardless of the market conditions.

So where do you find these key numbers that can help you assess the health of your own local market? Here are five ways to explore your local market without even leaving home!

Five Ways to Research Your Market

1. *Call a REALTOR.* The fastest way to find this information is to simply talk to a local real estate professional. As paid members of both the Board of REALTORs and the local Multiple Listing Service, REALTORs have access to in-depth market research, and most agents are happy to provide this information free of charge.

2. *Go online.* Many local Boards of REALTORs and Multiple Listing Services offer their market statistics to the public. In addition, many chamber of commerce organizations publish community statistics. Two new web sites that provide both consumers and agents with high-quality sales data are www.trulia.com (check out its heat maps!) and www.housingpredictor.com.

3. *Talk to the newspaper.* Most newspapers have a section devoted to real estate, and many update the local market statistics regularly. Try checking in at the paper or visiting its web site to find the latest real estate headlines.

4. *Talk to the assessor's office.* Local governments that tax private property have an assessor's office whose job it is to determine the value of real estate in the community. Often this office has detailed market statistics that are of public record and may be available in the office or online.

5. *Talk to an appraiser.* Appraisers are typically hired by banks to assess the fair market value of real estate. Because of this, appraisers must stay current on all of the local trends in the marketplace, and therefore they can be a terrific source of information.

So now that you have determined your motivation level and your local market conditions, it's time to put these pieces together to determine your strategy for success, which leads us to one of the first questions many home sellers ask themselves when considering putting their home up for sale.

Should You Hire a REALTOR or Sell on Your Own?

As a REALTOR myself, I would love to tell you that if you forgo the services of a real estate broker and sell on your own, the sky will fall or the world will end, but that's not true. Many homeowners successfully sell their homes themselves. In fact, according to the National Association of REALTORs, in 2006, For Sale by Owners accounted for 12 percent of the overall market (see Figure 1-4).

This may not seem like a large percentage, but when you consider that in that same year, there were over 6 million real estate transactions, this equals more than 720,000 sales without a REALTOR! It's enough to make a real estate broker like me want to have a good long cry.

One of the biggest motivators for private sellers is the possibility of saving the commission. To be honest, I can't blame them; I hate to pay a commission when I sell my own home, and I sell real estate for a living. And while data compiled by Real Trends, an industry information provider, shows

TOP THREE REASONS FOR GOING FSBO

- 51% did not want to pay commission fee
- 22% sold to a relative, friend, or neighbor
- 12% of buyers contacted seller directly

Source: National Association of REALTORs, 2006 Profile of Home Buyers and Sellers.

Figure 1-4

Method Used to Sell Home	
Sold home using agent or broker	84%
Seller used agent or broker only	80%
Seller tried FSBO first, then listed	5%
For Sale by Owner	12%
Seller sold home without agent	11%
Listed first, then sold themselves	1%
Sold home to home-buying company	1%
Other	3%

NAR 2006 Profile of Home Buyers and Sellers.

that commission rates have in fact dropped to an average of 5.1 percent nationwide, this still represents a $10,000 investment on a typical $200,000 home!

So why do we REALTORs charge so darn much money just to sell a home?

Before you go looking for a rope and my home address, let me explain. First, there is no set fee that real estate agents charge. Every broker, agent, or real estate agency has the right to charge what he feels his services are worth. Some charge a percentage, some charge a fixed fee, and a few charge an hourly rate. The pervasive myth that all real estate brokers charge a 6 to 7 percent fee to sell a home is simply not true; many charge more or less depending on the services they provide. Regardless of the size of the commission, let's take a look at where all that money goes (see Figure 1-5).

When you hire a real estate agent to market your home, you are hiring a listing agent. Likewise, when a buyer begins working with a real estate professional, she generally works with a selling agent to show her homes. So in the real estate business, there are two sides to every transaction, a listing side and a selling side. To pay for the services that the two agents provide to their respective clients, the commission is generally split between the two cooperating agents. So in

Figure 1-5   Where Does the Commission Go?

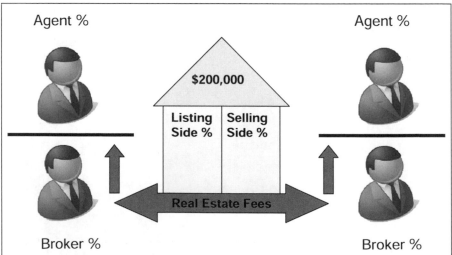

the case of our $200,000 sale, a 5.1 percent* commission rate would mean that each side of the transaction will receive roughly $5,100 (assuming that the agents split the fee equally).

So five grand is still a big chunk of change, right?

Yes, it is, but don't forget that most agents work under the umbrella of a broker. The broker's job is to provide a working environment for the agent, to oversee and manage the sales staff, to supervise the administrative staff, and, most importantly, to monitor the listing and escrow paperwork to stay in compliance with state laws. To pay for these services, the broker often takes a percentage or flat fee from every sale that closes. Although there are numerous commission arrangements between agents and their brokers, on average in the United States the real estate brokerage keeps 37 percent of the real estate commission and pays the remaining 63 percent to the agent. So in our example, this would mean that the agent would receive $3,213 at closing.

Hey, that's not a bad day's work, right?

Well, we're not done yet. In addition, the vast majority of real estate professionals are independent contractors. This means that they pay a large portion, if not all, of their expenses of doing business. How much does this total? On average, individual real estate agents spend another 13 percent of their income on everything from technology to marketing. In this transaction, that would mean they would need to set aside $417 to pay for their costs of doing business. So in the end the average agent's balance sheet on this transaction would look something like this:

Sample Agent Commission Breakdown

Sales price:	$200,000
Commission:	5.1%
Total =	$ 10,200
Selling office	–$ 5,100
Brokerage	–$ 1,887
Business costs	–$ 417
Net to agent	$ 2,796

---

*A 5.1 percent commission is used as a sample only and is not intended to be a suggested commission rate.

Now don't you feel sorry for us?

No? I wouldn't either. At the end of the day it doesn't really matter to you, the seller, how we split up our fees because the only number you see is the one that comes out of your proceeds at the closing table, and that number is huge. It's no wonder that many sellers decide to go it alone.

But before you grab your sombrero and head off on a trip to Cabo San Lucas with the savings from selling your home by owner, you might stop to consider that there will be significant costs involved in marketing your home that you wouldn't have with a real estate agent. For instance, without a real estate professional, you will no doubt have to absorb the costs of marketing your home, which might include ads in the local paper, open house signs, flyers, flyer boxes, real estate guide ads, and Internet marketing fees. For most homeowners, this number is likely to add up to 1 to 2 percent of the sale price and could be as high as 3 percent or more.

STRATEGY 3

Make informed decisions before hiring a REALTOR or selling privately.

Plus, there is the hassle factor. Take a look at Table 1-2, which gives a list of the things that private sellers consider to be the biggest hassles of going For Sale by Owner.

TABLE 1-2

Most Difficult Task for FSBO Sellers	FSBO (% of Respondents)		
	All FSBO	Seller knew buyer	Seller did not know buyer
Understanding and completing paperwork	17%	15%	18%
Preparing/fixing up home for sale	16	18	15
Getting the price right	14	16	12
Selling within the time planned	13	13	14
Attracting potential buyers	9	6	11
Having enough time to devote to all aspects of the sale	8	9	7
Helping buyer obtain financing	3	4	3
Other	20	19	20

So should you consider going For Sale by Owner?

One way to evaluate this question is to ask yourself if you would make a good real estate agent. I know this sounds a little crazy, since you may be trying to avoid hiring an agent. But think about it. What every For Sale by Owner does when he goes it alone is to take on the role of a seasoned real estate professional. He becomes his own agent. So would you hire yourself, or would you be better off hiring the real thing?

In training thousands of real estate professionals across the country, here are some of the qualities we look for in a top-notch real estate agent.

Top Five Qualities of a Great REALTOR or a Fantastic For Sale by Owner

1. *An eye for marketing.* The best real estate agents are often experts at marketing a home. They know how to write advertising, take high-quality photographs, and use software to produce high-quality flyers and advertisements. These skills are critical in attracting a qualified buyer.

2. *A people person.* The ability to talk with potential buyers and make them feel comfortable is one of the most valuable skills that real estate agents can possess.

3. *A powerful negotiator.* Often the most sought-after real estate agents are those who can successfully negotiate with even the toughest buyers and still create a successful win/win transaction.

4. *A good communicator.* Since the average transaction involves on average 12 different companies (even without a REALTOR), the ability to manage the flow of information is crucial to a successful closing.

5. *A detail organizer.* A real estate transaction is filled with a hundred little details that if missed can spell disaster. Successful agents are experts at managing these items and, more importantly, making sure they all get done.

When I survey the landscape of real estate agents and brokers across the country, the truth is that not all of them possess all of these qualities. But the best of the best, the superstars and top producers, the 10 percent of agents who sell 90 percent of the homes in America, by and large do, and frankly, these are the agents you will be competing with should you decide to go for the brass ring and try it on your own.

So now we're back to where we started: Should you hire a REALTOR or sell on your own? To help you answer these questions, check out the decision tree in Figure 1-6.

If you do decide to attempt to sell the home on your own, the good news is that you can find lots of help on the Internet to get your home sold.

Five Online Tools for Private Sellers

Hundreds of thousands of sellers just like you sold their homes last year, and collectively they saved millions of dollars in commissions. These people are homeowners just like you who put their pants on one leg at a time. So how did they do it?

One way is by taking advantage of tools that are now available on the Internet. For the private home seller, the Internet can provide a myriad of powerful tools that can help you sell a property without an agent. Let's take a look at five online tools that are becoming increasingly popular among For Sale by Owners.

Five Online Tools for Private Sellers

www.Owners.com. For a small fee, you can list your home in one of the largest online For Sale by Owner databases on the Internet.

www.craigslist.com. The largest online classified ad database in the world allows you to list your home for free on its web site and update the data as often as you like.

www.zillow.com. This web site allows any homeowner to research the home sales in her local market and get an estimated sales price for her home.

www.realflyer.com. Why build your own flyers when you can plug into preset online flyers and have them printed and shipped overnight?

www.base.google.com. With this Google tool, you can add your home to the mapping database in Google for free. This means

Figure 1-6 Should You Hire a REALTOR or Sell on Your Own:
Decision Tree

I want my home exposed to every possible buyer in the marketplace.

I need to sell quickly.

I've already found my dream home.

I don't have time to manage details.

I don't really want to deal with buyers.

I don't feel comfortable directly negotiating with someone.

I'm forced to sell.

My home is nice, but it could be a challenge to sell because . . .

I don't want to hassle with selling.

Yes, one or more of these statements describes me or my situation.

You may want to consider hiring a REALTOR.

OR

I already have a buyer in mind, and he has expressed interest.

I have plenty of time.

I want to be in complete control.

I don't mind showing my home.

I have no problem negotiating with people.

I will enjoy the challenge of marketing the home myself.

Yes, one or more of these statements describes me or my situation.

You may be someone who could be a successful For Sale by Owner that anytime anyone searches for a home in your area, your listing will be found on the map.

So with all of these new online tools, you may ask yourself, "Why should I even consider hiring a real estate agent?" It's a great question.

The Number One Advantage to Listing with a Real Estate Agent

Aside from having someone who can provide expert advice on everything from curb appeal to preparing a counteroffer, the key advantage that a real estate professional offers to a seller is access to buyers. Think of it this way: If you had the choice of putting your home in front of 10 buyers or 100, which would you prefer? Listing with a real estate agent almost always guarantees more exposure for your home, and more exposure means a faster sale at a higher price.

So why do real estate agents have an edge when it comes to exposing your home to the maximum number of buyers? Their first advantage is a huge sales force. When you hire a real estate agent, you don't just hire one agent; in essence, you put the entire Multiple Listing Service, which may include hundreds or even thousands of agents, to work. With your permission, these agents are able to show and sell your home in cooperation with your listing agent.

The second big advantage is that buyers prefer to work with a real estate agent. Put yourself in the buyer's shoes for a minute: If you're thinking about buying a home, would you rather open up the paper and search line by line for homes that meet your needs or go to a web site like www.REALTOR.com and see 90 percent of the residential listings in North America in a one-stop shopping experience? It's a no-brainer; the vast majority of buyers want the convenience of searching through a database of listed properties at their leisure. This is especially true for out-of-state buyers, who can account for up to 40 percent of the buyers in any market. These buyers rely even more heavily on the services of a real estate

> **STRATEGY 4**
>
> When considering your options, think like a buyer.

professional and the ability to instantly compare neighborhoods, market statistics, and even school districts online.

The question really boils down to this: Do the benefits of increased exposure justify paying the commission? Before you answer, let me give you one last statistic: According to the National Association of REAL-TORs, the median selling price of agent-assisted homes from mid-2005 to mid-2006 was $247,000 compared with $187,200 for For Sale by Owners—a whopping 24 percent difference. What does this mean? It means that in general, agents were able to not only help their clients recoup the costs of their fees, but also provide a net profit.

But if you're going to even consider hiring a real estate agent, who should you hire?

Discounter, Fee for Service, or Full-Service Broker—Which Should You Hire?

It may seem like a given that if you do decide to list your home with a real estate professional, you would work with someone who would provide you with a full range of real estate services. For instance, the top six services routinely requested by sellers are:

1. Help in selling the home within a specific time frame
2. Help in finding a buyer for the home
3. Help in pricing the home competitively
4. Advice on how to improve the condition of the home
5. Help with paperwork, inspections, and closing
6. Help with negotiation and dealing with buyers

Surprisingly, in many markets, sellers today have the opportunity to choose between receiving all of these services, some of these services, or even just one of these services. To decide what kind of company seems right for your situation, let's take a look at your most likely choices:

Real Estate Brokerage Models

Full-service company. The full-service brokerage is by far the most common type of real estate office. Generally, this type of real estate firm provides its clients with a complete range of real estate services, which often include help with marketing, positioning, pricing, and negotiating. In exchange for these services, the company charges a fee, generally a percentage of the sales price of the home, which it collects at closing. This is sometimes referred to as a *success fee* because in most cases this fee is paid only if the firm is successful in selling your home.

Fee for service. Fee-for-service real estate brokerages operate differently from traditional real estate companies in that these firms typically provide their clients with a menu of services. A seller can then choose from this list of services a la carte. Each service has an attached fee, which may be a percentage of the sale price, a flat fee, or in some cases an hourly rate.

Discount real estate company. This is best described as a real estate brokerage that offers services similar to those of a traditional company, but at a discounted rate. These firms often achieve operational savings through the elimination of costly office overhead by working virtually over the Internet or by putting limits on services like advertising and promotion.

Of course, when interviewing any real estate firm, it's wise to review the firm's service offerings, guarantees, and track record carefully before entering into a listing agreement. Although 73 percent of homeowners interview only one agent before listing their home, it's probably wise to consider interviewing a few agents to discover the best match for your specific needs and, just as importantly, to find an agent that you are comfortable working with; after all, when you list your home, you are really entering into a long-term relationship with this person.

Twenty Interview Questions to Ask Your Next Real Estate Professional

The truth is, most sellers hire an agent based not on his services, but on how the agent makes them feel inside. It's an emotional decision, not a logical decision. But is this the best way to go about finding someone to market your most valuable asset?

While obviously you want to be on friendly terms with your agent, what is far more important is the agent's ability to sell your home. Because of this, wise sellers go beyond an agent's ability to create trust and rapport, and dig deep into the list of services and track record that a potential agent can demonstrate. This ability to separate a personal from a professional relationship is a critical distinction that successful sellers have learned to navigate.

> **STRATEGY 5**
>
> When hiring a REALTOR, treat it as an interview.

One way to help this process along is to use a standard list of questions that you ask every potential agent.

Agent Questions

When interviewing any agent to list your home, it's wise to ask questions that will reveal the agent's ability to successfully accomplish your real estate goals. Here is a list of suggested questions:

1. How long have you been selling real estate?
2. How much real estate did you sell last year?
3. How many listings do you currently have?
4. Are you a full-time agent?
5. How many homes have you sold in my area?
6. What do you know about the market in my area?
7. What educational designations have you achieved?
8. What is your average market time compared to the market average?
9. What is your list price to sale price ratio compared to the market average?
10. How much are you willing to spend on marketing?
11. Do you farm my neighborhood?
12. Will you mail flyers of my home to the public?
13. Will you e-mail top agents about my home?
14. May I see a sample brochure of other listings that you have sold?
15. Do you provide a home book for prospects?
16. Do you provide a written report to sellers?

17. Do you have a personal assistant to help with details?

18. May I see your résumé or personal brochure?

19. If I list the home with you, do you have a specific marketing plan in mind?

20. How will you market my home online?

To be fair, you may want to provide your interviewees with these questions in advance so that they can prepare for the meeting and be able to put their best foot forward. (Unless, of course, you enjoy seeing people squirm, in which case, have fun!)

Whether you decide to market your home yourself or hire a real estate agent, by far the most important decision you can make in selling your home is setting the right price. So let's take some time to review this together in Chapter 2, "Setting the Right Price."

C H A P T E R 2

Setting the Right Price

The first question real estate professionals are often asked when visiting with a seller for the first time is: "What is my home worth?" No doubt this is one of your biggest concerns when deciding to sell your home as well. Obviously you don't want to set an asking price that is to low and leave money on the table, and likewise you don't want to set a price that is so high that your home never sells.

The challenge, then, is to set the right price relative to the market.

Believe it or not, there are actually three prices for every home. No, this is not a bad joke but an absolute truth. There is what the buyer would love to pay, there is what you as the seller would love to get, and there is what the home will eventually sell for. To prove it, I'll give you a personal example.

Several years ago, I purchased a two-bedroom home in a small town in Oregon for $75,000. It was a great buy. The home was an old-fashioned cottage with a stucco exterior, a carport, and a large backyard. After several years of renting the home, the time came for me to sell

> **THE THREE PRICES OF EVERY HOME**
>
> - What the buyer would love to pay
> - What the seller would love to get
> - What the home will eventually sell for

the property. I did some careful research and discovered that similar properties in the area were selling for between $120,000 and $135,000, depending on their location, features, and amenities. Logically, it would have made sense for me to price the property within this range. But, like most sellers, I had grown emotionally attached to the property. My little cottage was better than all of those other homes! It was cleaner, it had a better location, and, most importantly, it was mine!

So what do you think happened? Yes, I overpriced my own listing. I started the bidding on a Monday afternoon in the dead of summer at

STRATEGY 6

Avoid the temptation to overprice your home.

a mind-bending $149,000. *Hey*, I thought to myself, *if a buyer doesn't like my price, she can just make me an offer!* Instead, the home sat on the market like a rotten tomato for an entire month without so much as a showing. Finally I reduced the price to $139,000. And then guess what happened? You guessed it—again absolutely nothing. The property had become tired, stale, and boring. Every agent in the local real estate community had already pegged it as "overpriced." In desperation, four weeks later I slashed the price again, to $134,900, and then finally, in the middle of winter, I sold the dog for $125,000.

Now here's what's interesting: If I had been advising this knuckleheaded seller, I would have patiently explained that although starting high and working your way down the price ladder always sounds good on paper, in reality it can be disaster. Why? Take a look at the Seven Deadly Sins of Overpricing your Home.

The Seven Deadly Sins of Overpricing Your Home

1. Even if you do find a buyer who is willing to pay an inflated price, the fact is that over 90 percent of buyers use some kind of financing to pay for their home purchase. If your home isn't appraised for the purchase price, the sale is likely to fail.

2. Today's sophisticated home buyers are well educated about the real estate market. If your home is overpriced, they won't bother looking at it, let alone make you an offer.

3. When a new listing hits the market, every agent quickly checks the property out to see if it's a good fit for his clients. If your home is

branded as "overpriced," reigniting interest may require drastic measures.

4. Overpricing helps your competition. How? You make their lower price seem like a bargain.

5. The longer your home sits on the market, the more likely it is to become stigmatized or stale. Have you ever seen a property that seems to be perpetually for sale? Do you ever wonder: *What's wrong with that house?*

6. Buyers who do view your home may negotiate harder because the home has been on the market for a longer period of time.

7. You will lose a large percentage of buyers who are outside of your price point. These are buyers who are looking in the price range that the home will eventually sell for, but who don't see the home because your price is above their preset budget.

So how do you strike a balance between selling your home at a fair price and not feeling like you left a sack of hidden equity in the attic? Let's look at the secret to pricing your home to sell.

The Secret to Pricing Your Home to Sell

Contrary to popular belief, when you are selling your home, its value is determined by one thing and one thing only: what a qualified buyer is willing to pay for it. No more and no less. Sure, many sellers will argue that their home has an insurance replacement value, or an appraised value, or a tax assessed value, but unless your insurance agent, your banker, or your tax assessor is willing to write you a check for the home, guess what? None of that matters. A home without a buyer has no value in the marketplace. Sure, it might have a value to you the seller, and it might have a value to your banker, and to your insurance agent, and to your appraiser. But none of these people are buyers.

So here is the secret to pricing your home to sell: It's not what you think the home is worth that matters, it's what a reasonable buyer will think your home is worth that will ultimately determine whether your home will sell.

Now maybe you're thinking, *Hey wait. If I leave it up to a buyer, she will pay me as little as possible for my home.* True, she will. But in the real world, every buyer knows that you, the seller, have no obligation to sell your home at any price. To purchase your home, the buyer will have to make you an offer that you can't or won't refuse—one that will motivate you to pack up your Ken and Barbie collection, hire a local mover, and wave good-bye to a home full of memories.

But herein lies the trap that many sellers fall into (myself included), which is the mistaken idea that we can hold out for an inflated price and eventually the market will come to us. Wrong! Buyers are under no obligation to buy any particular home, and no amount of marketing, open houses, web sites, or signage will motivate a buyer to purchase an overpriced home. Why? Because he can buy one of your neighbors' homes for less! This reveals one of the most important considerations in pricing your home: price vs. time.

STRATEGY 7

Recognize that no amount of marketing will convince a buyer to buy an overpriced home.

Understanding Price vs. Time

The age-old dilemma that has faced buyers and sellers since the dawn of private property rights is a simple question: What is more important, price or time? Believe it or not, this conundrum underlies and controls every seller's decision to sell and every buyer's need to complete a purchase. For sellers, this boils down to the need to sell within a set time frame or instead to hold out for the best possible price, and as you might guess, for buyers, it's the need to buy within a set time frame or to purchase a home for the lowest possible price.

Looking at the matrix in Figure 2-1, you can see that a seller who would like to sell for top dollar should be prepared to potentially wait longer for a buyer who is willing to pay a premium price. It's like someone who is trying to sell ice in December; she might have to give the stuff away just to get rid of it, but if she can wait long enough— say, until mid-August when temperatures crest over 100 degrees— suddenly that same ice can have real value. On the flip side, a seller who needs to sell quickly and doesn't have time to wait should expect to discount his price somewhat because of the limited time he has to expose his home to the market.

What's the difference? Timing.

Figure 2-1   The Price vs. Time Solution

Sellers	Higher Price Longer Time	Lower Price Faster Time
Buyers	Higher Price Faster Time	Lower Price Longer Time

Motivation

Buyers are in the same boat. A buyer who has the luxury of shopping for a home over a long period of time can probably wait to find a bargain, while another buyer who must buy a home in the next few weeks will probably be willing to pay a premium. Again, it boils down to price vs. time. So you might ask yourself what is your highest priority: selling quickly, or selling for a higher price?

STRATEGY 8

Decide what is more important to you, price or time?

To be honest, when I pose this question to my own clients, they often smile coyly and then answer, "I want both!" The funny thing is that they aren't kidding. This sticky situation often reminds me of one of my first jobs after graduating from high school, which was working the graveyard shift at a local lumber mill. Like clockwork, the foreman would come by every night to monitor my production. We called him Perry, which could have been his last name or his first name because he never clarified it. Over the roar of the machinery, Perry would cup his hands together and yell, "You need to put out more wood!" Finally, after an especially tough day, I looked him back in the eye and yelled back, "Do you want quantity or quality?" Throwing his yellow hard hat down on the concrete floor and then kicking it for emphasis, he snarled, "I want both!"

Like Perry, most of my clients want their cake with the icing generously slathered on top. Because of this, many homeowners will attempt to put the responsibility for getting both top dollar and a fast sale on the back of their hired gun, the real estate agent. The result can be summed up in one word: frustration. Why? Because no matter how much a seller yells, screams, and kicks a real estate agent, that agent can't work miracles. This is why successful sellers understand that while a real estate agent's job is to provide marketing, expert advice, and negotiating services, in the end the agent doesn't own the property. She doesn't make the final decisions on pricing. The seller does, and ultimately the seller's asking price will in large part determine how slowly or quickly the home will sell.

To frame this discussion in a different way, consider what you will do if you arrive luggage in hand at the end of your listing period and the home has not yet sold. At that point, are you more likely to give it a little more time or adjust your price? I know: "Neither; I'll just fire the agent!" To be honest, this is exactly what many sellers do; they fire their agent and reboot the marketing. Does it work? Sometimes it does, but often these sellers end up three months later in the same slow boat to nowhere. Successful sellers, on the other hand, take ownership of their pricing decisions by making a clear decision about which is more important to them, selling quickly or selling for top dollar.

Once you have solved the mystery of whether selling quickly or selling for top dollar is more important to you, it's time to determine what a reasonable buyer will pay for your home. How? Often the best way is to understand and use a competitive market analysis.

Understanding and Using a Competitive Market Analysis

Successful sellers have learned that to price their home accurately, they need to think like a buyer; they need to get inside a buyer's skin and look at the world through a buyer's eyes. For instance, imagine for a minute that you are moving to another area of the country, to a city that you are completely unfamiliar with. If you were faced with buying a home in a strange city, what would be your first step?

If you're like most buyers you would probably start online by viewing listings at web sites like www.REALTOR.com or www.yahoo.com/realestate to get a general feel for local home prices. Next, you might narrow your search down to a specific community or neighborhood by comparing utility costs, school reports, and crime statistics, using other online tools like www.homefair.com or www

.neigborhoodscout.com. Next, as a typical Internet-empowered real estate buyer, you would look at an average of nine homes over eight weeks with the assistance of a real estate professional.

Like many buyers, by the end of your journey, you may have become so knowledgeable about the market that you can guess, with reasonable accuracy, each home's listing price before your agent can even tell you. So what happened? As a buyer, you went from being a blank slate, with no impression of the market, to having the ability to predict listing prices. That's a big leap, sure, but this is exactly what most buyers experience. But this is only the buildup; the next step for buyers who have found their dream home is to review a comparative market analysis.

A comparative market analysis is a report that compares a specific home, often called the "subject home," with other homes in a specific neighborhood. This analysis is then used to provide an anticipated sale price or price range for the subject property. Although not formally called an appraisal, the report provides a similar function by giving home buyers and home sellers a clear understanding of the market data that might affect their opinion of value. Because most of these reports revolve around comparing the subject home to several types of similar listings, let's take a look at the most common types of comparables.

> **STRATEGY 9**
>
> Use a CMA to identify what might influence a buyer's price opinion.

Common Comparison Properties

Active listings. These are homes that are for sale now that are as similar to the subject property as possible in terms of square footage, lot size, age, and construction. These homes are an important consideration, since buyers are likely to be viewing these properties in addition to the subject property before making a buying decision.

Expired listings: These are homes with characteristics similar to the subject home that failed to sell during their listing period. Why look at homes that failed to sell? Because this can often reveal problem areas that sellers may want to avoid, the biggest of which is overpricing.

Pending listings: These are homes that are currently under contract but have yet to close escrow. Often they can be a great indicator of how the market is trending. For instance, the National Association of REALTORs (www.REALTOR.org) profiles pending sales nationwide to gauge future sales activity.

Sold listings: These homes are by far the most important consideration in any comparative market analysis because they are those that actually closed escrow. Because of this, they demonstrate not what a seller hoped to get, or what a buyer would have loved to pay, but what the home eventually sold for.

To put these numbers to work, let's get our feet wet and take a look at a very simplified competitive market analysis. Our subject property is a two-bedroom, one-bath townhome built in 1986 (see Figure 2-2).

Figure 2-2

Single Family/Condo/Coop Property Comparative Market Analysis

Active Properties

Subject Property														
ML#	ST	Address	Town Name	List Price	RMS	BR	TBTH	Acres	LotSize	Gar	Bsmt	Yr Blt	List Date	DOM
1617464	A*	11 Brookline Court	Montgomery Twp.	$259,900	6	2	2.1	0.06	0.06	1	N	1986	6/21/2003	40
1620004	A	20 Andover Cir	Montgomery Twp.	$259,900	6	2	2.1	0.06	0.0634	1	N	1987	7/02/2003	29
1625152	A	42 Chicopee Dr	MONTGOMERY TWP.	$278,000	5	2	2.1	0.09	.09	1	Y	1980	7/27/2003	4
Average				$265,933										24

Pending Properties

Subject Property														
ML#	ST	Address	Town Name	List Price	RMS	BR	TBTH	Acres	LotSize	Gar	Bsmt	Yr Blt	List Date	DOM
1587687	P	9 Brookline Court	Montgomery Twp.	$249,900	6	2	2.1	0.06	.06	1	N	1986	2/06/2003	127
Average				$249,900										127

Sold Properties

Subject Property															
ML#	ST	Address	Town Name	List Price	RMS	BR	TBTH	Acres	LotSize	Gar	Bsmt	Yr Blt	Sale Price	Close Date	DOM
1584035	S	28 CHICOPEE DR	Montgomery Twp.	$244,700	6	2	2.1	0.06	2464 S.F.	1	N	1987	$244,700	3/17/2003	10
1597778	S	27 Chicopee Drive	Montgomery Twp.	$249,900	6	2	2.1		2760	1	N	1987	$256,300	5/27/2003	10
1611049	S	1 Brookline Ct	Montgomery Twp.	$249,900	6	2	2.1	0.06	2760	1	N	1998	$251,000	7/01/2003	13
1590096	S	5 Brookline Ct	Montgomery Twp.	$254,900	6	2	2.1		0.06	1	N	1986	$245,000	5/01/2003	42
Average				$249,850									$249,250		19

Because these townhomes have all been built by the same builder in the same community, almost everything about them is identical, with the exception of the amenities that the homeowners themselves may have added later.

The first set of properties listed in the report is the active listing group. These are the listings the seller will be competing with should he decide to sell. Notice that the average price for all of these homes is $265,933 and that they have all been on the market for an average of 24 days. The next group includes information on the one and only pending sale. This particular home has been on the market for over four months. Why so long? My best guess would be a condition issue, since the home seems to be offered at a discount compared to the other homes currently for sale.

The last group is the sold properties group. With the exception of one listing, all of the homes sold within two weeks of being listed. Why so fast? No doubt one of the biggest reasons is that the average selling price of $249,250 is substantially lower than the average price for the active listings. Does this mean that the active listings are overpriced? Not necessarily. In a seller's market, where homes are appreciating rapidly, it's likely that prices will steadily rise. In addition, every home is unique, and some homes may very well justify a higher price. But for practical purposes, let's assume that the subject home and the comparable listings are nearly identical. The big question, then, is: What is the right price for the subject property?

The answer is, it depends on the seller's motivation level (see Figure 2-3). For instance, if the homeowner is a necessary seller who absolutely needs to sell today, she might decide to go with a price that she knows has been paid before, like $249,900. Although this is not a guarantee of success, it is a safe bet that this price would attract any buyer who is considering a move into the community. On the other hand, an optional seller who is perfectly content waiting patiently for a buyer might join the other sellers by testing the market at a list price of $259,900.

But what if your home isn't a cookie-cutter

Figure 2-3

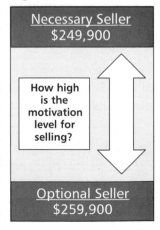

version of the other homes in your community? What if it doesn't fit neatly into a nice little box? Then it's time to understand the difference between objective criteria and subjective criteria when it comes to pricing.

Objective vs. Subjective Criteria

Consider for a minute what you would do if you decided to take your main squeeze out to dinner tonight. Of course, you have a ton of choices. You could take her out to a greasy spoon or a nice little bistro, or you could splurge and dine at a five-star restaurant. In making this decision, what will probably determine your choice more than anything is how recently you received your last paycheck. Why? As consumers, we expect to pay more for quality and uniqueness. The same is true with real estate. As home buyers, we expect to pay more for a home that offers more than just a basic floor plan and some stale French fries.

The challenge for a seller is settling on a price that takes these factors into consideration without overpricing the property. To do this requires gaining an understanding of the key differences between objective and subjective criteria. Let's take a quick look to get familiar with these terms.

Defining Objective and Subjective Criteria

Objective criteria. These are items that can be easily categorized and compared to other homes. For instance, things like square footage, number of bedrooms and bathrooms, heating systems, and lot size are all good examples of objective criteria.

Subjective criteria. These are items that are so unusual that it's unlikely that you can compare them to another home easily. Examples might include a breathtaking view, a unique location, or even a home's pedigree or ownership history.

To get a firm grasp of these concepts, let's look first at an objective criterion or, as we just learned, a piece of data that can be easily categorized and compared to other homes. A great example of this is a home's square footage, which can often be used to evaluate its potential sale price. For instance, a home can easily be compared

Figure 2-4

Pricing Your Home

Status	#	Average	Minimum	Maximum	Avg Sqft	Avg $Sqft
Active	2	$419,500	$389,000	$450,000	2292	$183
Off Market	3	$441,000	$425,000	$450,000	2336	$189
Sold	4	$416,188	$389,750	$475,000	2325	$179
Total Listings	9	Sold Properties closed averaging **96.79%** of their Final List Price. This reflects a **3.21%** difference between Sale Price and List Price. If SNL status is included, the Sold Price to List Price ratio will be affected because the ratio is always 100% for SNL listings.				

to other similar homes on a square footage basis by simply dividing the sale price of each home sold by its respective square footage. To see this in action, take a look at Figure 2-4, a sample competitive market evaluation prepared by Denny Austin of All State Real Estate (www.allstaterealestate.com) in Roseburg, Oregon.

Notice that in this CMA, Denny has used active listings, off-market (another way to say expired) listings, and, of course, sold listings. Furthermore, he has broken down his report to include an analysis of each category by square footage. With this information, using a pocket abacus, any homeowner can quickly calculate an estimated sale price. For instance, if the subject home is 2,200 square feet, the numbers would reveal:

Average sold price: $393,800 (2,200 square feet × $179)

Average listed price: $402,600 (2,200 square feet × $183)

(We could also calculate the price based on properties that went off the market, or expired, but since these sellers were unsuccessful, it may not be helpful to follow their pricing example.)

So how about the big remodeling job you did last year to add a bedroom or a bathroom? How much will that increase the value of your home? According to *Remodeling Magazine's* 2006 Cost vs. Value report, "A home improvement project costs only 20 cents to 25 cents on the dollar. The other 75 cents to 80 cents spent on a project goes directly back into the home through increased value—not to mention increased owner enjoyment."

You can actually purchase a specific Cost vs. Value report for your area, and in many cases your city, by visiting www.costvsvalue.com.

These reports will provide a detailed breakdown of the value (or lack thereof) of any recent additions, changes, or modifications you have made to your home. In appraiser speak, this is sometimes known as making adjustments. In other words, you start with a base price like the one we just calculated for our 2,200-square-foot home and then adjust the price based on the home's unique characteristics. One important note about making adjustments is that the knife can cut two ways. In other words, adjustments aren't always positive and quite frequently can be negative. A good example of this is a home that has many years of deferred maintenance. Obviously this home can't be evaluated solely on its square footage; the price has to be adjusted to take into account its current condition.

> **STRATEGY 10**
>
> Be careful of over-adjusting your price to compensate for features or flaws.

So how much do you add or deduct? That is a subjective decision, one that is made based on the experience and perceptions of the person doing the evaluation. While a homeowner may tend to gloss over his home's flaws, a buyer will see these details with a critical eye. The reverse of this is true as well; for instance, a seller may feel that his view is "worth a million dollars," while a buyer may just shrug her shoulders.

If your home includes positive or negative subjective criteria, you may want to rely on the expertise of a certified appraiser or a real estate professional to give you an unbiased opinion of what your home's unique features might add to (or subtract from) the sales price. Of course, when interviewing real estate agents for the job of selling your home, you want to be careful that the agents don't enter into a bidding war.

Avoiding a Bidding War for Your Listing

Imagine that you have invited three real estate agents to come by your home to provide you with a presentation of their services and give you an opinion of the value of your home. As each agent arrives, he gives you the standard song and dance about what he can do and why you should hire him. All of them are freshly scrubbed behind the ears, with good suits and nice shoes, and as they talk, they all seem friendly. But let's be honest: The only thing you really want to hear is the price.

In the distance, drums beat, horns blow, a chorus of singers triumphantly reaches its highest note, and finally, finally, the agent arrives at the suggested price page of his analysis. The crescendo has arrived! The climax of the interview!

How much is it? Will it match your dream price, the price that will allow you to retire early, buy a Rolex, and take that long vacation to the Greek islands?

For many sellers, this is how they feel when talking to a real estate agent about the potential sale price of their home: as if the fate of the whole world rests on the opinion of one real estate agent. But this can be a huge bear trap. To demonstrate, let's take a look at Figure 2-5, which shows a group of real estate agents' presentations to Tom, a typical homeowner.

If you were Tom, which agent would you choose? Most sellers like Tom would choose the agent that tells them the highest price, in this case Agent A. Because of this, many sellers find themselves in a bidding war; in other words, agents have a natural tendency to move away from their own professional opinion toward a higher and higher price in order to secure a listing. In the real estate business, we call this buying the seller's love. Why would a real estate agent do this? For the same reasons that you tell your kids that their pencil drawings are works of art. You crave your kids' affection, just as a real estate agent craves your acceptance and thereby your listing.

Figure 2-5 Real Estate Agents Competing for a Listing

Agent A	Agent B	Agent C
I think the home will sell for $395,000	I think the home will sell for $375,000	I think the home will sell for $350,000

STRATEGY 11

Don't buy into a
bidding war.

Successful sellers don't base their decisions on which agent tells them the highest price; instead, they carefully study each agent's analysis and then form their own overall opinion. They take ownership of the pricing decision. It is, after all, your home, not the agent's. To aid you in this decision-making process and to parse out what an agent is really thinking, let's take a look at using the truth serum technique.

Truth Serum: Giving Real Estate Agents Permission to Tell the Truth

Agents often need to be given permission to unleash their brutal honesty. You can help by having a quick discussion with them before they offer their pricing thoughts. For instance:
Seller: *Before we talk about price, I want you to understand that I don't want you to tell me what you think I want to hear. I want you to tell me the truth. I need to know what you honestly think I can sell this home for and how you came to that conclusion. It doesn't mean I'll agree with you, but I want you to know that I'm not basing my listing decision on who tells me the highest price.*
Does that sound fair?

In addition to this simple strategy, you might also use the technique that banks often use when listing a foreclosed home. Many of these firms require an agent to provide not just one price opinion but several opinions based on different criteria. For instance, they may ask for a price opinion based on:

• Selling the home in 30 days, 60 days, or 90 days
• Selling the home in its current condition or an improved condition
• Selling the home with buyer incentives or without buyer incentives

By considering different pricing scenarios, wise sellers can begin to tap into the power of strategic pricing, a technique that top real estate agents commonly use to ensure that their listings sell faster and for top dollar.

Strategic Pricing—Using the Magic of Price Points

When buyers walk into a real estate office and sit down with an agent to begin searching for homes, they do something very predictable. They pick two price points, as in, "We would like to look at homes between $200,000 and $225,000." Why? Because it's simple, neat, and clean. Even if their lender has told them that they are qualified to purchase a home up to $229,400, inevitably they will just round that down to $225,000 or round it up to $230,000.

Because of this tendency of home buyers (and real estate agents) to round up or down by five- or ten-thousand-dollar increments, successful home sellers often use what I call price points as a way to gain maximum exposure for their home. How do they do this? They slightly adjust their listing price to a more strategic price, a price at which more buyers are likely to see their home. To understand this concept, it's important to understand how a real estate agent uses the Multiple Listing Service database (MLS) to search for homes.

STRATEGY 12

Use price points to gain maximum exposure.

The first step for a real estate agent sitting with a recently qualified buyer is to talk about the buyer's price range; as we mentioned earlier, the top and bottom of the range are typically rounded up or down to the nearest price points and then entered into the MLS search engine (see Figure 2-6). Once the search criteria have been entered into the system, the program instantly sorts through every available listing, and within seconds returns a list of the properties that fall within the required parameters (see Figure 2-7).

Figure 2-6

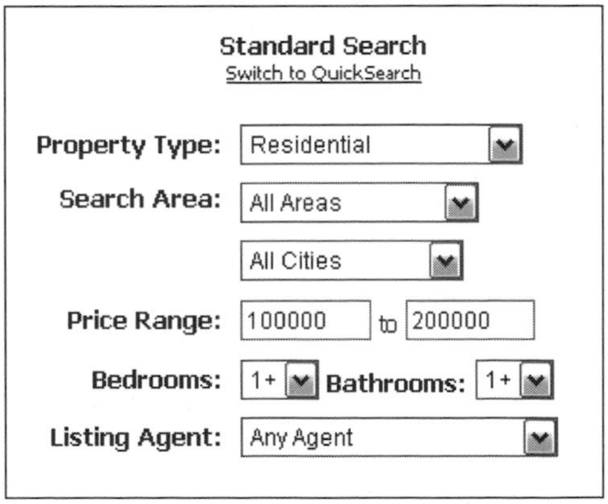

Standard Search
Switch to QuickSearch

Property Type: Residential
Search Area: All Areas
All Cities
Price Range: 100000 to 200000
Bedrooms: 1+ Bathrooms: 1+
Listing Agent: Any Agent

A common misconception among home sellers is that all buyers are automatically exposed to their home just because it's listed in the MLS database. Not so. The only time a buyer will see your home is when it falls between the two price points that the buyer has set as his minimum and maximum acceptable price. Keeping this in mind, let's take a look at how wise homeowners use price points to their advantage:

Seller Price	Strategic Price Point	Major Price Point
$307,000	$305,000 or $310,000	$300,000
$283,500	$280,000 or $285,000	$275,000
$196,000	$200,000 or $195,000	$200,000
$512,000	$510,000 or $515,000	$500,000

Let's start by looking at the first example, a seller who wishes to price her home at $307,000. The problem with this price is that a typical buyer looking at homes probably isn't going to say, "Let's look for homes from $292,000 to $308,000." So pricing a home at $307,000 doesn't make a lot of sense. Instead, a strategic price for this home would be either $305,000 or $310,000. By making this simple adjustment, any homeowner can help keep her listings in the sweet spot for buyer searches.

Figure 2-7

Now you might notice that there is another category for this home, called the major price point. A major price point is any $25,000 price increment. Major price points are important to recognize because these are generally the diving boards that buyers and agents spring their home searches from initially and then slowly ratchet up from later. To stay with our first example, a buyer probably wouldn't start a search by looking at homes that are priced at $305,000 or $310,000. Instead, most buyers, at least in the beginning, would say, "Let's look at homes priced at $300,000 and under." Because of this, a seller who wants to secure a sale quickly may consider adjusting her price down to the nearest major price point.

Now for something really controversial. How many times have you heard the urban legend about a seller who, after unsuccessfully marketing his home, actually increased his price and then, bingo, sold the home? To be honest, as a real estate professional, I always think, "*Yeah, right.*" But the truth is, it can happen. How? The seller probably hit a more active price range. By researching which price ranges in your market are the most active, you can fish for buyers in the best market holes. For instance, take a look at these sample data:

Price Range	Number of Sales, January–June
$200,000–$225,000	162
$225,000–$250,000	97
$250,000–$275,000	104
$275,000–$300,000	173

Obviously the most active price range for this particular market is the $275,000–$300,000 price range. Now I know it goes against the grain of traditionalist thinking, which says to always price a home based on its individual merits compared to other similar homes. But this often ignores the overall market reality. For instance, might it be wise for a seller who was considering pricing his home at $270,000 to move up to the next major price point of $275,000? It makes sense to me if there are significantly more sales in that price range. Of course, this works both ways; for instance, a seller who was considering a strategic price of $230,000 may be wise to move down a category and price her home at $225,000. Why? For the same reason—it's a better pricing strategy.

Still another consideration in setting the right asking price is the overall market curve. Are prices headed up or down, and how should that affect your asking price?

Pricing Ahead of the Curve— How to get Ahead of the Market

Now what if your market is trending quickly down or quickly up (see Figure 2-8)? Can this affect your pricing strategy? Of course. In both

Figure 2-8 Is It a Rising or a
Declining Market?

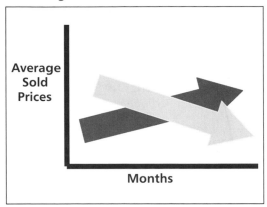

cases, you might miss an opportunity to sell your home for top dollar if you do not keep a careful eye on the market trends for your neighborhood. In a rapidly rising market, for instance, it might be wise to look very closely at the pending sale prices and the active listings, not just the sold properties. Based on this, a savvy seller might want to consider pricing her home more aggressively, knowing that if she is slightly above the market, in a very short time the market will catch up.

But what about the reverse, a declining market? You might think of a declining real estate market as being like a stock market sell-off. In a bear stock market, what tends to happen is that sellers chase the market down. In other words, they keep agreeing to lower and lower prices just to lock in what little profit they may have left. Believe it or not, the same is often true in a bear real estate market. Sellers chase the market, first by rushing to put their homes on the market, thus causing a buildup of inventory, and then by slashing their prices just to get their homes sold.

This is a dangerous position for any seller. For instance, in a declining market, even if you price your home competitively, within a few days or weeks your price maybe significantly higher than what more motivated sellers are asking for their homes.

Take a look at how easily this can happen with Suzy Homeowner.

> **Suzy would really like to sell her home in the next 60 days, but of course she wants to net as much money as possible from the sale. Studying her competition and relying on the advice of her real estate professional, she lists her home for $345,000.**

Based on this price let's take a look at Suzy's competitive position today:

Competitor Home A:	$368,000
Competitor Home B:	$349,000
Suzy's Home Today:	$345,000
Competitor Home C:	$345,000
Competitor Home D:	$333,000
Competitor Home E:	$329,000

Suzy appears to be very competitively priced relative to the market. But let's see what happens 30 days later:

Competitor Home A:	Expired
Suzy's Home Today:	$345,000
Competitor Home B:	$339,000 (reduced price)
Competitor Home C:	$335,000 (reduced price)
Competitor Home D:	Sold
Competitor Home E:	Pending
Competitor Home F:	$326,000 (new listing)
Competitor Home G:	$325,000 (new listing)
Competitor Home H:	$319,000 (new listing)

Wow! What a market transition! Suzy went from being very competitively priced to being the highest-priced property within her price range. As a buyer, which home would you look at last? This is a terrible position to be in, and the scary part of this scenario is that in most cases a seller like Suzy would never know it. Why? Most sellers request a market analysis only at the beginning of a relationship with a real estate agent. Instead, wise sellers make sure to request an updated list of comparable listings every 30 days! To take control of your home sale, you must be proactive. One way to be proactive is to understand what to do when nothing is happening.

STRATEGY 13

Review your pricing position every 30 days.

Price Adjustments—When and How Often?

The day has come! You've listed your home for sale, and now you're so excited you can hardly stand it. You've done the research, checked out the competition, and priced your home competitively. So it should just be a matter of time now, hours even, before your first buyer arrives. The house is immaculate (it should be after your marathon cleaning session over the weekend), ready for a buyer to take the grand tour. So you sit by the phone waiting for the first call to come.

Two days go by with nothing. Not a showing, an e-mail, or even, from what you can see through the curtains, a drive-by. Where are all the buyers? You've checked the home's web page a thousand times; it looks perfect. The advertisement in the Sunday paper looks great, too. The flyers in the flyer box are full color with both interior and exterior photographs, but none of them have been taken. Your home is not selling.

Guess what? Your home is overpriced.

The first barrier buyers must overcome before viewing a home is the price. If a buyer cannot get past the price, if that wall is too high, the home will not be shown. This means that you can have gold-plated showers and diamonds embedded in the drywall, but it still won't matter. Why? If no one comes to see your home, its condition—good or bad—doesn't really matter. An inescapable truth, then, is that if your home receives no showings, this almost always means that your home is overpriced. So what can you do about it? You can wait for the market to catch up with your price, which can takes months or even years, or you can be proactive and adjust your price to meet the market.

But how much should you adjust the price?

This is a great question, and the answer is very simple: To have any effect at all, you must adjust your price by a minimum of one price point. To give you an example:

Current Price	Next Strategic Price Point	Major Price Point
$299,000	$295,000 or $290,000	$275,000
$274,900	$270,000 or $265,000	$250,000
$196,000	$195,000 or $190,000	$175,000

While any price reduction is better than nothing, the problem with a tiny price reduction is that in all likelihood it will have almost no effect on the number of times the home is shown. Why? Because in most cases the seller will not have brought the price down enough to reach beyond the same group of buyers who have already seen the home. To gauge how deep to make the incision, sellers must first decide where they want to be positioned relative to the competition. For instance, suppose today your home was priced at $595,000, but the competition was spread all over the playing field like this:

Subject Home:	$595,000
Competitor A:	$579,000
Competitor B:	$578,500
Competitor C:	$578,000
Competitor D:	$577,500

You might decide that a reduction to $590,000 would have little or no effect on the home's ability to attract a buyer. Instead, a proactive seller might decide that to be competitive, the price would need to be reduced to at least $580,000, and possibly as low as $575,000. Of course, this is often a big sticking point with sellers, who will say, "But I've already come down from X price." But come down from what? A price you would have never received? This is often what's known in the real estate business as the difference between fantasy and reality.

For instance, a seller could ask $1,000,000 for a home that is worth only $250,000. Clearly this is a fantasy price. Realistically, in order to sell the home, the seller would have to reduce the price by at least three quarters of a million dollars. To the homeowner, this might seem like a huge price reduction—but only because he is failing to consider that the home was massively overpriced to begin with.

So is it better to do one big price reduction or several smaller ones?

It depends on your motivation to sell. Some sellers have found that a steady stream of small price reductions can signal to buyers and agents that they are slowly bleeding out and possibly becoming desperate to sell at any price. Obviously this can put a seller at a disadvantage when it comes time to negotiate a sale. Because of this, many sellers find it more advantageous to make as large a price adjustment at one time as they can stomach. Why? Resetting the price in a more dramatic way can often spur instant activity and create more excitement about the home.

After considering the market factors that will affect the price of your home, what should you do then? You should start thinking about marketing plans that will get potential buyers interested in your home, which means that it's now time to dive into Chapter 3, "Promotion—Fishing for Buyers."

C H A P T E R 3

Promotion—Fishing for Buyers

Selling your home is a lot like fishing. You have to find where the buyers are hiding, attract them with the right bait, and then reel them in. Easy enough, right? You would think so, but unfortunately, many sellers do everything perfectly up until the time they put their pole in the water. In other words, they price their home competitively, get their home in the best condition possible, and even offer incentives, but then, surprisingly, they still go home with an empty stringer. Why? They haven't mastered the art of fishing for buyers, or what we call in the real estate business promoting the listing.

Promoting your home in the real estate marketplace means that you place your home in front of as many qualified buyers as possible. But don't worry, this isn't as daunting a task as many homeowners might imagine; in fact, with a few tips, any homeowner can soon be landing the big marlins. To start, let's look at Table 3-1, which gives the ways most buyers find their dream home.

TABLE 3-1
WHERE BUYERS FIRST LEARNED ABOUT THE HOME THEY PURCHASED

Real estate agent	36%
Internet	24%
Yard sign	15%
Friend/neighbor/relative	8%
Home builder	8%
Print newspaper	5%
Knew the seller	3%
Home book or magazine	1%

*According to National Association of REALTORs, *2006 Profile of Home Buyers and Sellers.*

Real estate professionals and successful homeowners understand that attracting the maximum number of buyers means using the right lures, and according to these NAR findings, one of the best tools for attracting buyers is an old-fashioned yard sign.

Signage—Five Ways to Make Your Sign Stand Out

Believe it or not, a real estate sign, after a real estate agent and the Internet, is the single most effective tool for attracting a buyer to your home. Why? A good real estate sign is like a marketing machine that's hard at work in the rain, snow, sleet, and sun 24 hours a day, 7 days a week. Still, as good as real estate signs are, I have a pet peeve about them that drives me absolutely bananas. What is it? It's when a seller or an agent places a "For Sale" sign parallel to the road. Take a look at Figure 3-1.

As I was told by one of my first real estate mentors, buyers aren't owls. They won't turn their head at a right angle to see a real estate sign. You have to make it easy. "Turn your sign so that it faces oncoming traffic and your sign calls will triple," my mentor explained, and he was right. Once I began turning my signs so that they were perpendicular to the road, my buyer calls jumped dramatically.

But don't stop there! To help create the most effective sign strategies for your home take a look at these five tips:

1. *Place your sign as close to the road as possible.* The closer your sign is to a buyer's line of sight, the greater the chances that the buyer

Figure 3-1 Which of These Signs Will Buyers Notice More Often?

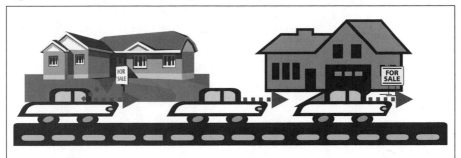

Real estate signs are more effective when they are perpendicular (facing the traffic), rather than parallel (facing the other side of the street).

will see it. You may need to check with your local city planning office regarding the placement of a "For Sale" sign, as some cities and even some homeowners' associations prohibit or put limits on sign placement.

STRATEGY 14

Ensure that your real estate sign has maximum visibility.

2. *Place your sign in a clear line of sight*. Test your sign's effectiveness by driving by your house. Make sure that your sign can be seen from a distance and that it is not blocked by trees or shrubs. Also, before making a sign investment, check out several different sign styles by visiting web sites like www.realestatesupercenter.com.

3. *Make sure phone numbers are easy to read*. A buyer may have only a few seconds to see and remember your phone number. Make the print large enough for buyers to see the number clearly from the road. Some sellers and real estate agents even purchase vanity phone numbers that are easily remembered. Also, make sure that the sign is clean—this means giving it a good wipe-down every weekend.

SELLING BY OWNER: WHAT'S YOUR NUMBER?

Buyers want immediate answers when they call about a home. Choose a phone number that you or your spouse will be able to answer at all times, or at the very least respond to very quickly. Some sellers even tap friends or relatives to field calls if they are unable to handle buyer inquiries during the day.

Figure 3-2

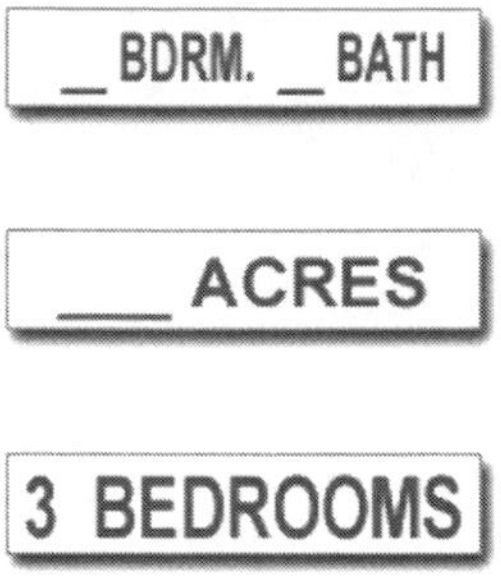

4. *Use sign riders.* A sign rider is a small sign attached to your main sign that describes features of the home (see Figure 3-2). It's a sign for your sign. Why use a rider? Using one or two riders can pique a buyer's interest. But be careful; agents and owners who overuse riders can easily end up with a sign that looks like a pitch for a carnival attraction. Two to three sign riders is generally the limit.

5. *Use directional signs.* Directional signs (see Figure 3-3) point to your home's location from the surrounding side streets. This will increase the number of buyers who will know that your home is for sale, which is important, as many buyers start their real estate searches by doing "drive-bys."

Figure 3-3

In my own real estate company, we have found that during peak seasons, sign calls can account for as many as 30 percent of inbound calls. Yet, surprisingly, some sellers still ask to forgo a sign. Why? They want to keep their listing a "secret" from their neighbors. My question to these sellers has always been: "Won't the neighbors know the home has been sold when the moving van arrives?" What's the big secret?

Homeowners who are truly committed to selling use every tool in their arsenal to attract a qualified buyer. One tool that many progressive agents and sellers use is a device that allows their home to become a "Talking House."

Figure 3-4

(((((((Talking)))))))
House.
The High-Tech Listings & Leads Program

Talking Houses: Letting Your Home Speak for Itself

Imagine that as a buyer, you are driving through a neighborhood, and you stumble across a home that strikes your fancy. In front of the home there is a traditional "For Sale" sign, and another sign that says "Tune your radio dial to 1260 AM to learn more about the home." Curious, you park across the street and adjust your radio dial until you find the station.

This is what you hear:

> "Thank you for looking at 300 Richmond Ave. This home is a custom-built three thousand square foot home featuring four bedrooms, a den, a game room, and daylight basement. The home has been remodeled to include granite counter-tops, cherry wood cabinets, and new carpets. The home shows pride of ownership, and has been meticulously maintained throughout. . . ."

The recording goes on for another couple of minutes and then invites you to take a private tour of the inside of the home. Would you be impressed? Many buyers are impressed and do take the next step to schedule an appointment.

STRATEGY 15

Consider using technology to allow your home to speak for itself.

Called a Talking House (see Figure 3-4), the device, about the size of a small stereo, stays in your home and broadcasts a prerecorded message on any AM station that you specify. The signal can be heard for up to 3,000 feet. To use a Talking House system, many homeowners list their home with an agent who offers the device as a part of his services. Though the company doesn't sell the product directly to For Sale by Owners, it does provide a list of agents who are willing to rent the systems, for as little as a few dollars a day. To learn more, you can visit the company's web site at www.talkinghouse.com.

Figure 3-5

For Generations X and Y (home buyers in their twenties and thirties), another increasingly popular option is the use of cell phone text messaging technology to deliver real estate information (see Figure 3-5). One company that is at the forefront of this new high-tech information delivery system is www.property4cell.com.

How do these systems work?

It's simple. When a buyer drives by a home that she wants more information about, she calls the phone number listed on the sign rider for more information. At the prompt, she types in a text message code, and instantly she is given the home's basic details, along with an invitation to speak directly to the listing agent or to make a showing appointment.

Of course, regardless of whether you choose to use a Talking House or a text messaging service, no seller wants a buyer to leave his home empty-handed. This is one reason why so many sellers insist on using a flyer box.

Flyer Boxes—The Great Debate

Once you have planted a "For Sale" sign in your lawn, one decision that you will need to make is whether you want to use a flyer box. A

Figure 3-6

flyer box, like the one pictured in Figure 3-6, is a plastic case or envelope that generally hangs from a traditional "For Sale" sign and is used to distribute promotional flyers.

There are two schools of thought about flyer boxes. The first is that flyer boxes are the greatest thing since Post-it notes, since a buyer who likes your home will be able to obtain additional information about the property instantly (while her interest is still peaking). The flip side of this argument is that buyers who receive all of the information they need from a flyer may have no reason to call a real estate agent or a private seller because they already have everything they need to know.

Let's assume you buy into the first argument. You want a flyer box. No problem; just make sure you keep it stocked with flyers. Nothing irritates a buyer more than finding a home she likes, stopping her car, unbuckling her seat belt, crossing

> **STRATEGY 16**
>
> When using a flyer box, keep it fully stocked with flyers.

the street, and reaching inside a flyer box—only to find it empty. To avoid this pitfall, try one or all of these three tips to keep yourself and your real estate professional honest:

Fun with Flyer Boxes

1. *The head count technique.* Count out 25 flyers and place them in your flyer box. Once a day (or more often, if needed), replenish the supply of flyers by adding just enough to bring the total to 25 flyers. This will tell you roughly how fast your flyers are being picked up and how many flyers you should keep on hand.

2. *Stack them.* If you're working with a real estate agent, ask him to supply you with an extra hundred flyers to keep inside your house. You can then resupply the flyer box as needed.

3. *Weatherproof them.* Damaged flyers are of no use to anyone. Make sure that your flyer box can withstand the local weather. For some areas this might mean having a box that can hold up under snow or rain, while in other areas it might mean being able to withstand high winds.

Whether you choose to use a flyer box or not, there's no doubt that in marketing your home, you will probably want to use a flyer. A promotional flyer is a great way to highlight your home's best features and give buyers a small taste of what to expect when they come inside your home.

Nine Tricks to Building Flyers That Create Excitement!

Take a trip down memory lane with me. Remember the first time you viewed your home? It was a magical experience, wasn't it? No doubt you had a list of reasons why the home would make the perfect place to live, things that you rattled off to your friends and family in excited, breathless sentences.

Now, of course, you just want to be rid of the darn thing! But wait; you need to get back in touch with what turned you on about your house in the first place, the things that fired you up, raised your blood pressure, and made you stay awake at night. Why? So that you can sell that sizzle to the next buyer.

FEATURES VS. BENEFITS

Feature:
A specific item of value that a home may offer.

Benefit:
What the item of value does for the client.

STRATEGY 17

When building flyers, highlight the features and benefits of your home.

One place to start is by identifying your home's best features and benefits. What is the difference between a feature and a benefit? A feature is a specific item of value that a home may offer, while a benefit is what that item of value does for the client. For instance, your home might feature unique architecture, interior design, lighting, or amenities that would be considered special features. What those items do for a buyer are called benefits; for instance, perhaps they provide a breath-taking skyline, open space to entertain friends, or a relaxing atmosphere. Savvy sellers and agents focus on highlighting the benefits of each feature, not just the feature itself. For instance, look at these two sample bullet point lists:

THIS HOME FEATURES:

- Covered deck
- Three-car garage
- In-ground sprinklers

This typical list of home features is accurate, but pretty boring. Sure, the bullet points describe the home accurately, but what they don't do is describe what the features will do for a buyer, in other words, why a buyer should care.

THIS HOME FEATURES (WITH BENEFITS):

- Covered deck—for a relaxing summer barbecue!
- Three-car garage—room to park all of your toys!
- In-ground sprinklers—set it and forget it!

In this example, the seller has described not only the features, but also the potential benefits of those features—the reasons why a buyer should care. Think of this as painting a picture. The buyer should see himself already living inside the home, enjoying the amenities that the home offers. We often think buyers will do this automatically. Not true. Successful sellers often have to jump-start a buyer's imagination, to get him thinking and visualizing himself in the home.

Now that we know what we're selling, let's explore what else you can do to create a powerful flyer, one that blows the doors off of your competition. Let's look at nine tricks for building powerful flyers.

Nine Tricks for Building Powerful Flyers

1. *Create an engaging headline.* A headline is what will grab a buyer by the coattails and drag him into the content of your flyer. Make sure that your headline is engaging and you will be 90 percent of the way to creating a successful flyer. (More on this in the next section.)

2. *Less is more.* A buyer who is given too much information will disregard the entire advertisement. So, narrow your story down to the home's best selling points. If you keep it short and simple, buyers will be far more likely to read the entire flyer and take action by calling you.

3. *Include multiple photos.* Buyers want multiple photos. They want to see more of the home, not less. In a study conducted by the California Association of REALTORs, it was found that the most frequent request among buyers in real estate marketing was to include more photos.

4. *Include contact information.* Make it easy for buyers to take the next step by including accurate and easy-to-find contact information. This includes a daytime phone number and an e-mail address.

5. *Use full color.* Buyers respond to color. Plus, it's far easier to highlight and contrast information using different colors. This is backed up by a study conducted by Joan Meyers-Levy and Laura A. Peracchio in the *Journal of Consumer Research*. They found that consumers were far more responsive to color advertising, especially when doing a quick review of information.

6. *Use a professional layout.* You can download flyer templates at www.microsoft.com and other paid web sites like www.classified flyerads.com. These professionally created layouts will dramatically improve your flyer's appeal and avoid the homemade mistakes that are so easy to make.

7. *Use font styles sparingly.* Be careful of using multiple font styles in one flyer. According to graphic design expert Jennifer Krynin, follow these simple rules:

   • Don't use more than three or four fonts on any one page.

   • Don't change the font in midsentence.

   • For printed fonts, good choices are Arial, Geneva, Helvetica, Lucida Sans, Trebuchet, or Verdana.

8. *Use the right size font.* If you make the font on a flyer too small, it can be hard to read. With the exception of the headline, a 12- to14-point font should be the right size for most flyers.

9. *Use proper grammar and spelling.* Nothing distracts a buyer faster than poor spelling or bad grammar. Even the best word-processing programs can miss common grammar and spelling mistakes, especially on a flyer layout. Wise sellers have their flyers proofread before printing.

Now let's take a look at a sample flyer (Figure 3-7) and identify all of these points in action.

Building a high-quality flyer is critically important to any seller's successful marketing campaign. But once you have created your masterpiece, how will you know if it's right? One way to test your new design skills is to use the AIDA approach.

The Secret System for Creating "Can't Miss" Marketing

If you were to come to me as a seller, flyer in hand, and ask me to evaluate your flyer, or for that matter your ad copy or your home's web site, my first step would be to apply a simple system called the AIDA approach. It's not new. In fact, the AIDA approach to marketing is something that every college marketing student learns in her first semester at school.

Figure 3-7

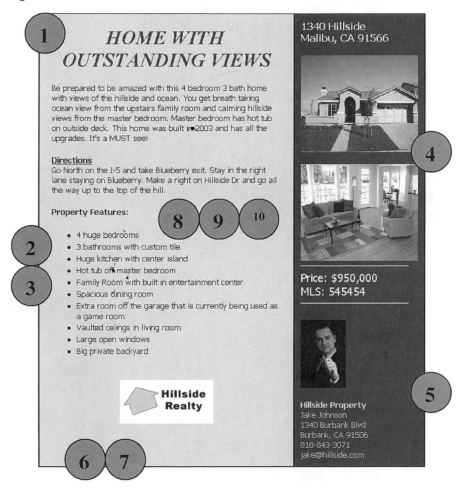

Unfortunately, this technique is a secret to most sellers, and even to many real estate professionals. Why? Most homeowners and agents have never been trained to use this technique. This means that while they are struggling to build marketing pieces that connect with buyers, you can apply the AIDA approach to create marketing pieces that will stand up against even the toughest competitors in your market. To tap into the AIDA

STRATEGY 18

Always measure your marketing against the results it produces.

approach, let's first break down the letters to grasp their full meaning. AIDA is an acronym for:

A: Attention

I: Interest

D: Desire

A: Action

Attention: Standing Out in a Crowd

To truly stand head and shoulders above the competition requires something bold, sensational, thought-provoking, or at the very least interesting. In other words, smart sellers always start their marketing by understanding the need to grab people's attention. One powerful example of this is the headline of your advertising.

Headlines are said to be read ten times more than the body of any advertisement. Just consider the last time you were in a grocery store checkout line. Did you read the magazine headlines? Not just the funny ones like the *Weekly World News* ("My Babysitter Has Three Heads"), but all of the other periodicals screaming for your attention. Did any of them make you stop and purchase the magazine so that you could read more? Perhaps it was *Newsweek*, *Time* magazine, or *USA Today* that was competing for your attention. But the real question is, who won? If the answer was nobody, then those magazines lost an opportunity; they did not stop you dead in your tracks.

This is what I call gut-level marketing. Great marketing must first hit you in the gut. It's not a logical response; contrary to popular belief, consumers don't study advertisements, weigh the benefits versus the costs, and then, after careful consideration, decide to continue reading, watching, or listening. Instead, audiences either like the ad or not, usually within just a split second of their exposure to it. It's an emotional experience, purely gut level.

In addition to a great headline, another powerful way to stop readers dead in their tracks is to use the power of pictures. Pictures have the power to convey a message far faster than any group of words. Why? People think in pictures, not words. Consider the last time you had a dream; did you dream in words or in vivid, streaming visual images?

So how can we use pictures in our real estate marketing? Take a look at the sample flyer in Figure 3-8 and how the agent uses pictures to generate interest. Not only does this agent provide a picture of the front elevation of the home, but he also includes photos of the interior and the backyard as well. This mini-tour approach can be very effective in building excitement about viewing your property.

Figure 3-8

HOME WITH OUTSTANDING VIEWS

Be prepared to be amazed with this 4 bedroom 3 bath home with views of the hillside and ocean. You get breath taking ocean view from the upstairs family room and calming hillside views from the master bedroom. Master bedroom has hot tub on outside deck. This home was built in 2003 and has all the upgrades. It's a MUST see!

PROPERTY INFO
Property Address:
1340 Hillside
Malibu, CA 91566

MLS: 545454
List Price: $950,000

CONTACT INFO

Hillside Property
Jake Johnson
1340 Burbank Blvd
Burbank, CA 91506
818-843-3071
jake@hillside.com
Visit My Website

Hillside Realty

PROPERTY FEATURES
- 4 huge bedrooms
- 3 bathrooms with custom tile
- Huge kitchen with center island
- Hot tub off master bedroom
- Family Room with built in entertainment center
- Spacious dining room
- Extra room off the garage that is currently being used as a game room

- Vaulted celings in living room
- Large open windows
- Big private backyard
- 2 Fireplaces - 1 in family room and master room
- Auto-sprinklers in front and back
- Beautiful landscaping
- Balcony off family room and master room

PROPERTY PHOTOS

OTHER INFORMATION
Go North on the I-5 and take Blueberry exit. Stay in the right lane staying on Blueberry. Make a right on Hillside Dr and go all the way up to the top of the hill.

Interest: Holding a Buyer's Attention

Homeowners can't afford to have their home viewed as just another commodity, another home in a long list of homes that buyers can choose from. Instead, successful sellers find ways to separate their home from the market, to show off the differences. Ask yourself: How is my home unique compared to the competition? Try looking at things like location, architectural features, construction details, remodeling projects, and landscaping. Also, don't overlook soft amenities. Soft amenities are those items that may be intangible but that add real value to your home's desirability. Examples of soft amenities might be a desirable school district, proximity to shopping or medical services, or even a nearby neighborhood park.

> **DON'T FORGET THE SOFT AMENITIES!**
>
> Soft amenities are items that may be intangible but that add real value to your home's desirability.

THE POWER OF GREEN HOUSING TO HOLD A BUYER'S INTEREST

For eco-friendly buyers, a "green" house can be just the ticket for grabbing their attention and holding their interest. But what is a "green" home? According to the U.S. Green Building Council (www.usgbc.com), based in Washington, D.C., it is defined as a home that incorporates features that result in:

- Using less energy
- Using less water
- Using fewer natural resources in construction
- Creating less waste
- Having better indoor air quality

While only 0.3 percent of all homes in America are now considered green, defined as having at least three of the five elements listed here, the 2006 Residential Green Building Smart Market Report predicts that by 2010, the value of residential green homes will rise to $38 billion.

To find an agent who can leverage your green home, you may want to look for an agent who has earned the eco-broker designation. To find an agent near you, visit www.ecobroker.com.

Desire: Overcoming Buyer Resistance

Now, you have stopped the client dead in her tracks by grabbing her attention, and you have successfully held her interest by offering her something unique. The big question is: Is the client now going to pick up the phone and call you? Maybe or maybe not; the key determinant in this decision-making tree can often be something called buying resistance.

Think about the last time you made a large purchase. Just as you were about to max out your gold card, did something creep into your mind? What many people suffer from at this point is buying resistance. Buying resistance is that nagging voice in the back of your head that keeps whispering to you that you should think longer, shop harder, and avoid making a buying decision.

Buyers need to feel comfortable about making the decision to call a real estate agent or owner about viewing a home. They don't want to feel trapped into a high-pressure sales pitch; they just want to view the home and then decide if they want to move forward. To overcome this natural reluctance, many agents and sellers have learned to use some simple yet powerful techniques.

Three Ways to Overcome Initial Buyer Resistance:

1. *Offer prerecorded information.* Many sellers and agents invest in a voice message system, often available through your local phone company, that will enable you to record a message providing detailed information about your home that buyers can tap into 24 hours a day, 7 days a week.

2. *Offer access to a virtual tour.* A virtual tour is an online walk-through of your home that buyers can view from the comfort of their home. This allows buyers the luxury of snooping through your bedrooms and bathrooms without ever picking up the phone. (More on this technique later.)

3. *Offer easy showing options.* Let buyers know that viewing your home is easy. If your home is listed, you might note that the home can be shown by using a lockbox. If the home is unlisted, you might note the days or times that the home is available for showings.

Action: Motivating a Client to Call You

The ancient Greek mathematician Archimedes, long regarded as one of the most influential scientists of all time, is credited with the famous conclusion "Give me a big enough lever and I can move the world." Archimedes discovered that massive weights can be moved with a relatively small amount of force by using the power of leverage. Believe it or not, we can apply this same principle to building a real estate flyer.

Think of a buyer's motivation to take action as a block of concrete, something that is massively heavy and almost impossible to move. Any homeowner can inspire a buyer to pick up the phone (or mouse) by using the right lever. The challenge, then, is to identify the right lever, because, of course, every buyer is motivated by different things. Because of this, many successful home sellers use an ideal client model. An ideal client model is the seller's perception of what the most likely buyer for his home will look like, not physically, but demographically.

When you create a picture of your most likely buyer, many things will fall into place. First, you will be able to build your marketing around a specific target audience—something that professional marketing experts always do before launching any new product. Second, you will be able to identify what is likely to motivate this buyer to take action. For instance, if you believe that your buyer is likely to be a retired couple, featuring the proximity to local golf courses, community services, or even college campuses in your marketing might be the lever that produces results. Finally, when placing advertisements, you may be able to identify what these buyers are likely to be reading, watching or listening to.

Here are a few questions to get you started:

> **STRATEGY 19**
>
> Market your home to a specific audience by building an ideal buyer model.

The Ideal Buyer Work Sheet

1. What demographic age group does your ideal buyer fall into?
2. Is the buyer married? Does she have children?
3. What income bracket does the buyer fall into?

4. What is her educational background?

5. Has she bought or sold a home before?

6. What kind of occupation(s) does your buyer have?

7. What is your buyer's net worth?

8. What are your buyer's hobbies?

9. Is your buyer tech-savvy?

10. Does your buyer own investment real estate or a second home?

Is this an exact science? No. Marketing is never an exact science. As when bowling blindfolded, successful home sellers aim their marketing in the right direction, use the best techniques possible, and then throw their best shot. They may knock down six pins, roll a strike, or end up with a gutter ball, but then, like everyone else, they get to try again. An ideal client model greatly increases your odds of success. But before you strap on your wrist guard and begin your famous twinkle-toe maneuver, it's important that you understand the myth of print marketing.

The Myth of Print Marketing

Print marketing doesn't work. It's a complete waste of time and money. Why? It's highly unlikely that a buyer who sees your home in the paper will actually end up buying your home. You don't believe me? According to the National Association of REALTORs, only 6 percent of buyers learn about their home from traditional print marketing: 5 percent from the local newspaper, and another 1 percent from local real estate guides.

So why do real estate agents and brokers continue to spend literally hundreds of millions of dollars on print marketing every year when they know full well that print marketing will probably never produce the buyer who eventually buys your home? It's simple. They're afraid that if they don't, you won't list your home with them. According to a study conducted by *Classified Intelligence* and

STRATEGY 20

Accept the idea that in most markets, print marketing doesn't work unless you modify your approach.

Realty Times in August 2006, "REALTORs tell us that they're still buying print—not because it works better than other ad choices, but because sellers expect to see their listing in the local paper as proof that their agents are working for them."

Unbelievable! I know, you're right, it is unbelievable. But guess what? I do the same thing every day. Why? Because I have a trick up my sleeve, actually four of them, that enables me to beat the odds and produce results where others fail. Interested? Great. Let's look at the first one, which is tapping into emotion.

Tap Into Emotion

In writing print advertising copy, many sellers and agents fall into the trap of attempting to squeeze every single one of their home's amenities into the available space. Because of this, they end up writing ads that look like someone spilled a bowl of alphabet soup. Take a look:

> **Grab Your Hat!**—This TH has it all: 3br/2bth and a blt wbs in the mstr. Don't miss the cac and frog. The gmt kitchen will make you glad you have a fdr. Call Jim today at 555-1212.

Buyers don't carry a pocket real estate translator with them when reading real estate advertising, so it's important that you make it easy for them to decipher your home's benefits and features. The actual advertisement, if written in plain English, would look like this:

> **Grab Your Hat!** This town house has it all: 3 bedrooms, 2 bathrooms, and a built-in wood-burning stove in the master bedroom suite. Don't miss the central air conditioning and finished room over the garage. The gourmet kitchen will make you glad you have a formal dining room. Call Jim today at 555-1212.

Equally dangerous is the "pack it" technique used by many agents and builders. The idea here is to list as many homes as possible within a budgeted space. To do this, homes are often reduced to little more than single lines of data. The real problem with both of these approaches is that they make the assumption that buyers are interested only in dissecting information, that they buy homes based only on logic. They don't. Buyers ultimately buy homes because of the way a home makes them feel. It's purely emotional. Yes, they use logic to eliminate properties, as in *I only want a four bedroom*, or *I want a home in the Ridgeline Estates*. But they connect with and buy a home based on emotion. It's like picking a new puppy. You eliminate the canines that are

HOMES FOR SALE

3br/2bth split level, pool, westside—$330,000

2br/1bth condo, remodeled, vacant—$195,000

5br/2bth view home, exclusive area—$496,000

2br/2bth cottage, vintage, cute—$245,000

the wrong age or the wrong breed by establishing your logical parameters. But once you get down to the nitty-gritty of choosing the pooch that will be in your home for years to come, you look for that special bond, that emotional connection that lets you know that you have made the right choice. The same is true in real estate advertising. Successful home sellers write ads that tap into a buyer's emotions.

Let's look at a couple of examples:

Light Your Barbecue. Life will be sweeter while relaxing on a deck overlooking the city lights. The deck comes with a two-level, 2,000-square-foot home complete with a home theater room and a custom gourmet kitchen, perfect to show off your inner chef. Come experience a new lifestyle. Only $595,000.

Do you like S'mores? Bring your marshmallows and cozy up to the fire. This home features a river rock fireplace, a lodge-style interior, and an old-fashioned front porch. Invite your friends because the spacious 1,800 sq ft of living space offers two master bedroom suites, and a hot tub! Call today, only $299,000.

Both of these advertisements are designed to create a visual image, a picture in the buyer's mind that goes beyond his logical defenses and instead touches his emotional center. Of course, one argument that can be made about this style of ad writing is that the copy is generally longer and thus will be more expensive to run. That's true. But which would you rather have: a cheap ad that doesn't work, or a slightly more expensive ad that does? It's a no-brainer. Wise sellers understand that cost is only relative to effectiveness. Another trick to enhancing your effectiveness is to target multiple buyer groups.

Target Multiple Buyer Groups

It's quite possible that your home will have not just one type of likely buyer, but two or even three distinctly different demographic groups whose members might be willing to write you a check at closing. Because of this, many wise homeowners build one, two, or even three different kinds of marketing plans, each designed to appeal to a different demographic group.

For example, a home that might be considered a starter home could also be considered a perfect home for a couple that is downsizing or retiring. Because of this, a seller who makes the mistake of focusing all of her advertising on first-time home buyers may miss an opportunity. To avoid this scenario, let's take a look at how a seller attempting to sell a condominium in Portland, Oregon, might target multiple markets.

TARGETING MULTIPLE MARKETS

Advertisement 1: Targeting Relocating Buyers

Move In Today? This upscale condo in the heart of Portland offers buyers immediate occupancy. With a split-level design, a master bedroom big enough to fit your king bed, and oak wood floors, you will feel at home in the Northwest. Now walk out on your deck and catch a view of the Columbia River! Priced to sell quickly at $495,000.

Advertisement 2: Targeting Move-Up Buyers

You've Earned This! You deserve the lifestyle this exclusive condo in the heart of Portland can offer you. From sweeping views of the Columbia River to a luxurious master bedroom suite and oak wood floors, this split-level home says that you have made it! Priced to move at $495,000.

Advertisement 3: Targeting Downsizing Buyers

A Turnkey Lifestyle? Forget the weekend projects! This luxury condo offers a near-maintenance-free lifestyle in the heart of downtown Portland. Offering a spacious split-level floor plan, a large master bedroom suite, and oak wood floors, this home is a rare find. Add in a view of the Columbia River and you have a dream property. Won't last long at $495,000.

By writing three different advertisements, each targeting a different buyer group, agents and homeowners can dramatically expand their potential buyer pool and increase their odds of securing more showings.

A side benefit of this approach is that rotating your ad copy will keep your home from getting stale. How many times have you seen the same ad copy for a home repeated for days or weeks at a time? Having three different advertisements that rotate will enable your listing to appear fresh and new every day. But before you take the step of placing your advertisement, make sure that you rejection-proof your ads.

Rejection-Proof Your Ads

Buyers are machines, supercomputers who can move through a newspaper classified section within minutes, red pen in hand, slicing and dicing each listing in their quest to find a dream home. What's worse, buyers don't look at real estate ads for reasons to accept your home; they look for reasons to reject it. Why? Intuitively they know that there is such a vast number of properties available that they have to find a way to quickly eliminate as many properties as possible from consideration. To deal with this dilemma, buyers will find any reason to kick your home to the curb by picking out key words or phrases.

Fortunately, there is a solution. Successful homeowners carefully craft ads that eliminate as many potential red flags as possible. They rejection-proof their advertising. Let's take a look at this technique in action:

TYPICAL ADVERTISEMENT

Bake a Cake? Yes, it's time to celebrate! This 1,200-square-foot ranch-style home in Santa Cruz offers 3 bedrooms and 1½ baths. The single-car garage is perfect for hobbies, and the small fenced yard is a great place to enjoy the sunshine! Only $895,000.

Notice that in this advertisement, the seller has used some details that could cause a buyer to reject the home; I count at least six. For instance, a buyer looking for a 1,300-square-foot home might reject this home because it appears too small. Likewise, a buyer looking for a home with two baths may throw this home out because it is listed as having only 1½ baths. Also, the home's location could be used against it, as could the use of the word *small* in describing the yard.

Now many sellers might ask, "If my home doesn't fit a buyer's parameters, why do I want her calling me?" It's a valid question. The answer is that buyers are far more flexible than they let on. While they may start with a set of seemingly rigid requirements, these often soften as their search continues. For instance, a buyer who originally would accept only a home with two baths might very well come to accept one with 1½ baths; likewise, a buyer who was previously set on 1,300 square feet may decide to accept a 1,200-square-foot home. As a seller, you can't afford to miss those opportunities.

Let's take a look at a variation of this same advertisement, after it has been rejection-proofed.

REJECTION-PROOFED ADVERTISEMENT:

Bake a Cake? Yes, it's time to celebrate! This spacious ranch-style home, located in a beautiful seaside town, offers a picture-perfect setting, along with ample bedroom sizes, an attached garage, and a fenced yard. Don't miss this bargain. Priced to sell at only $895,000.

While this ad is far more general, it is also far more likely to generate buyer calls. When writing your own ad copy, look at your advertisement from the standpoint of a buyer. The harder it is to reject your home, the better the job you have done. But even a rejection-proofed ad can be ineffective if a buyer can't find it, which is why the location of your ad is so important.

Location, Location, Location—Placing Ads Where Buyers Can Find Them

The words "location, location, location" don't just apply to buying and selling real estate; they also apply to where you place your real estate advertisements. The better the location of your advertisement, the greater the chances that a buyer will discover and purchase your home.

STRATEGY 21

Don't throw money at marketing; choose each venue carefully.

So how do you determine where to invest your marketing budget? One way is to study what successful real estate agents are already doing. Agents invest thousands of dollars a year in marketing their listings, and because of this, they tend to find the best places to generate the maximum number of buyer inquiries on their listings.

To ensure that you're making a smart choice, when deciding where to invest your marketing dollars, always request a media kit. A media kit will contain details about the audience, age range, and economics of the group watching, listening to, or reading the marketing venue. Many companies now provide their media kits as a download from their web site. Also consider that how often an ad runs can have a great impact on its effectiveness. Obviously an ad that runs only once will not reach as many buyers as an ad that runs three times over a week. The more often you throw your hook into the water, the more likely you are to attract a buyer. Of course, there is one hook that buyers just can't resist. It's something that will make every advertisement you do get noticed. It's the power of pictures.

> **MEDIA KITS**
>
> A media kit will contain details about the audience, age range, and economics of the group watching, listening to, or reading the marketing venue.

Four Ways to Take Picture-Perfect Photos

Home buyers love pictures (see Figure 3-9). Why? They don't have to waste time reading anything. Instead, they can just zoom through pictures, like mug shots, until they find one they like. Pictures don't lie. They also don't puff, or spin, or even sell. They don't say "cozy" when they mean small, they don't say "easy maintenance" when they really mean no yard, and they never say "vintage" when they really mean fixer-upper.

Looking at a picture gives buyers the sense that they are getting the real story. Because of this, most buyers, when given a mix of adver-

Figure 3-9

STRATEGY 22

To help your home stand out, use high-quality photos.

tisements including plain text ads and picture-enhanced ads, will almost universally skip the text ads and jump right to the pictures. Like being a dandelion in a field of roses, if you don't have a photo attached to your ad, no one will notice you. On the other hand, if you really want your home to stand out, you can use pictures to your advantage. Professional photographer Carson Coots of Houston, Texas, offers these helpful hints:

Pick the right tools. Using your old Polaroid to take photos of your home won't work, as most media outlets today request that you submit your photos digitally. For a complete review of the best digital cameras on the market, check out www .consumerreports.org. *Advanced tip:* To capture the highest-quality digital images, set your camera to the highest pixel and compression settings possible.

Exterior daytime. For the best possible photos, take into consideration the lighting and the direction that the house is facing. The sun rises in the east and sets in the west, so consider which direction the house faces when scheduling a time to shoot. For daylight photos, you will want the sun behind you (see Figure 3-10). Advanced tip: To make sure the sky is a deep blue and the clouds (if any) are clearly defined, try using a polarizing filter.

Figure 3-10

Exterior evening. A nice evening photo can set your home apart when it comes to advertising. A photograph taken right at dusk, with a slower shutter speed and the right lighting, can transform almost any home into a castle (see Figure 3-11). *Advanced tip:* To light

Figure 3-11

your home, try using 500-watt shop lights, positioned at opposite ends of the house, and a long exposure time to capture as much light as possible.

Interior photos. Interior photos are a terrific way to show off your home's best amenities (see Figure 3-12). Although midday is not a great time for outside photos, it is ideal for interior photos, because the light will not be shining right into the windows. *Advanced technique:* Experiment with shots using both ambient (natural) lighting and a flash.

Figure 3-12

A well-taken picture can make the difference between your home attracting a buyer's attention and becoming a real estate wallflower. If you're a photography buff, knock yourself out; if not, it may be a good idea to follow the lead of many real estate superstars who hire a professional photographer to make their listings come alive.

So now that you have created a masterpiece of marketing brilliance, it's time to sit back and let the phone ring. But what do you say when a buyer actually calls?

Four Secrets to Converting Calls into Showings

Buyers call real estate agents and private sellers for a reason. They want something, namely information. For instance, a buyer who has seen your advertisement in the local newspaper might call you to find out the address of the property, while a buyer who has seen your lawn sign might just want to know the price of the home. In either case, the buyer needs something from you. That's why he's calling. As soon as you deliver this information, nine times out of ten the buyer will hang up and you will never hear from him again.

To avoid this fate, many top real estate agents employ a system called the *commodity exchange*. The commodity exchange starts with the premise that as a real estate agent or private seller, you hold something, a commodity, that is precious to the buyer: a piece of information that the buyer wants to know. As soon as the buyer extracts this commodity from you, her need to continue the conversation ends. For example, check out a typical buyer call to a real estate office:

Agent: Hello

Suspect: I am calling about the house in the paper. Your MLS number is 23453; it's got a price of $230,000. Can you tell me the address?

Agent: Sure, just give me a minute here. . . . Yep, it's on Johnson Street.

Suspect: What's the address?

Agent: It's 124 Johnson. Hey, listen, are you working with an agent? Hello . . . Hello . . . Hello . . .

To take back control of the conversation and to set an appointment for a showing, agents and owners must establish an exchange rate. Your exchange rate is what you will ask for in return for handing over information about your home.

> **STRATEGY 23**
>
> Be ready to handle buyer calls by using a script.

The more information you can extract from the buyer, the more likely it is that you will be able to learn her housing motivations. Why should you care? The more you know about a buyer, the easier it is to focus your conversation on a buyer's hot buttons or what the buyer is most interested in finding in her next home. This dramatically increases your odds of converting the call into a showing.

So what should you require from a buyer? What should your exchange rate be? As a starting point, it would include the buyer's name and phone number, and then widen from there as you continue the conversation. To demonstrate, let's take a look at two simple scripts:

> **CALL CONVERSION AD CALL**
>
> **Suspect:** I'm calling about your ad . . .
>
> **Owner:** Great. We've had a lot of interest in the property. My name is <your name>; what was your name? [answer] Could I also get your phone number, just in case? <answer>

Suspect: I wanted to know <question>.

Owner: No problem. But before I tell you <answer>, can I ask you a couple of questions?

Suspect: Sure, I guess . . .

Owner: Can I ask where you saw the advertisement? What attracted you most to the advertisement? <Answer>

Owner: You know, our home has <describe benefits and features related to buyer's interests>, but listen, instead of my trying to tell you about the house over the phone, how would you like to come by and take a quick tour? Would this evening be good for you, or would tomorrow work better?

This script allows the seller to take control of the conversation by first asking for the buyer's name and phone number and then digging deeper by exploring what attracted the buyer to the advertisement in the first place. Of course, you will get the occasional tight-lipped buyer who won't want to give you his name and phone number. At that point, you have two choices: You can cut bait and tell him to take a hike, or you can give up your commodity. My recommendation: Don't give in; tell him that without this basic information, you don't feel comfortable giving out information over the phone. Giving away information about your home is, after all, a security issue, something that even the most easygoing homeowner should be very careful of doing without at least having basic information about a buyer.

Now let's take a look at another script, this time with a buyer who has driven by the home:

CALL CONVERSION SIGN CALL SCRIPT

Suspect: Hello, I'm calling about a sign . . .

Owner: Great; we've seen several people driving by the house over the last few days. My name is <your name>, and what was your name? <answer> Could I also get your phone number just in case? <answer>

Suspect: I want to know <question>.

Owner: Sure, no problem, but can I ask you a couple of questions first? <Pick two or more>

What did you like about the house?
Are you looking for a home with < >?
Do you live here in . . . ?
Do you own a home now?
Do you need to sell before you purchase?
Have you already spoken with a lender?
How long have you been looking?

Owner: You know our home has <describe benefits and features related to buyer's interests>, but listen, instead of my trying to tell you about the house over the phone, how would you like to come by and take a quick tour? Would this evening be good for you, or would tomorrow work better?

You might notice that in this script, the seller has been a little more assertive by asking qualifying questions. Qualifying questions are questions that reveal whether the buyer has not only the motivation to purchase a home, but the ability as well. This may seem a little forward at first, but for the savvy seller, it is far better to ask these questions now rather than after a showing has been scheduled.

To be prepared to handle your next buyer inquiry, try following these four easy strategies:

1. *Use a script.* Take the time to map out your conversation. If you follow a pattern in your call conversion process, you will build strong habits. As unnatural as this may feel in the beginning, you will become more at ease with them as you handle more and more calls.

2. *Track your success.* Measure your success against your actions. Is your script working? Can you make improvements? Are you setting appointments?

3. *Use simple conversion tools.* Keep copies of your advertising close at hand, keep a pad and paper nearby, and always keep your appointment book open and ready.

4. *Listen, practice, and rehearse.* To ramp up your call conversion skills, try practicing your scripts with everyone in your home who may be fielding calls. Also, you may want to invest in a digital tape recorder and begin recording your side of buyer calls. Although this will be

excruciating to listen to, you will be able to shake out problems that are preventing you from converting calls into closings.

Now for a topic that can sink a traditional homeowner's marketing boat faster than a rogue wave—marketing to the new Internet-empowered consumer. So are you ready to tap into your inner geek? Great! Because it's time to jump into Chapter 4, "Web Marketing."

CHAPTER 4

Web Marketing

Can you imagine a time, somewhere in the not too distant future, when you will sit down at your computer, view a few homes, take a couple of virtual tours, and then, like buying a vintage Beatles album, point and click to complete the purchase of a new home?

No?

Good, because I can't either. Buying a home isn't like booking a vacation or buying the latest Stephen King novel. A home is a unique commodity, something that can't be easily packaged and sold over the Internet. Buyers want to experience a home in person; they want to see it, touch it, and even smell it before they make an offer. Of course, that doesn't mean that parts of the home-buying process haven't been "webized," or broken down into smaller pieces that can be done very efficiently online. One of those pieces is the home search, or the process of narrowing down a buyer's choices from thousands of potential homes to just a small handful.

As many sellers have discovered, today's tech-savvy buyers often won't bother to pick up a newspaper or real estate guide; instead, they will opt for the faster and far easier option of searching for their next home online. In fact, according

> Nearly three-quarters of all buyers conduct their home searches online.

to the National Association of REALTORs *2006 Profile of Home Buyers and Sellers,* nearly three-quarters of all buyers today conduct their home searches online. Because of this, successful sellers understand that marketing their home online isn't optional; it's an essential strategy for exposing their home to the entire marketplace. So how do you make sure that your home won't be the last pair of socks at the bottom of the Internet bargain bin?

The easiest way to do this is to employ a real estate agent who already has a strong online presence. Real estate professionals invest heavily in technology, with 71 percent of agents reporting that they have a personal website devoted to helping buyers find homes. Of course, the burning question is: With so many agents online, how do you know which ones are truly Web marketing experts? To find out, try using the SOLD acronym to narrow the field:

> **STRATEGY 24**
>
> Choose a real estate agent who is tech-savvy.

Are You SOLD on Your Next Agent?

S: *Search engine placement.* Buyers who are searching for a home will generally begin their searches by finding a website through a search engine. Search engines rank a website based on a combination of factors. In theory, the more popular the site, the higher the site will be ranked. Try using www.google.com or www.yahoo.com to identify the real estate companies and agents that rank the highest.

O: *Options.* Buyers want the ability to search not only an individual agent's inventory but the entire market. They want to see it all, everything. Because of this, many agents and brokers employ IDX, or Internet Data Exchange, technology to share not only their own listings but the entire Multiple Listing Service (MLS) database with potential buyers. To ensure that an agent is using IDX, test each agent's website. Can you see the entire market or only the agent's own listings?

L: *Listing enhancement.* Buyers are information vampires. They want to drain every drop of information they can from a website. Agents who provide only cursory or basic information about their listings are often passed over in favor of meatier, more content-filled sites. To avoid this fate, wise agents provide enhanced information on each of their listings, things like more photos, more detailed descriptions, and even virtual tours.

D: *Delivery speed.* Online buyers are notoriously impatient. How fast an agent responds to e-mail inquiries can often determine the agent's chances of winning a buyer's business. Try testing your prospective agent by sending an e-mail question about one of her listings. If she takes more than three hours to respond, it could be a red flag that she doesn't have the internal systems in place to handle a buyer's questions promptly.

As a real estate broker myself, my website is something that I believe sets me apart from the competition. I'm proud of it. If you give me a chance, I'll even tell you all of my impressive website statistics, like how many hits, page views, unique visitors, and downloads are tracked on my website each month. But how do you know I'm telling you the truth?

You don't unless you do some homework. One easy way to do some discreet detective work is to use a website popularity index like the one found at www.alexa.com. By simply typing the name of any website into the index, you can find out how well the site is doing based on several different indicators, including overall popularity, reach, traffic rank, and page views. But a word of caution: I've met many new and experienced agents who were fantastic at building (or buying) compelling websites, but who failed miserably in the field. Great agents have to be great both online and offline. They must be able to step out from behind the keyboard and sell. A real estate agent who can't sell is like a surgeon who can't operate; no amount of marketing can fix the problem. Interview several agents and quiz them about both their online and their offline selling strategies.

Once you have narrowed the field down to a few agents who have both the technology skills and the selling skills to get your home sold, it may be a great time to discuss MLS marketing.

MLS Marketing—Five Ways to Maximize Showings

Amazingly, what most homeowners and even many real estate agents don't realize is that their most effective online marketing tool is almost always the local Multiple Listing Service

STRATEGY 25
Use the MLS as a marketing tool for maximizing exposure.

(MLS). In many markets, as many as half of all sales are cooperative sales, or sales in which the listing agent cooperated with another agent who brought in the buyer. In some markets, even private sellers can enter their homes into the MLS database for a small fee.

The MLS system is the clearinghouse where real estate agents store data about their listings. Most MLS systems have two sites, a password-protected site for real estate agents and an open public site. The public site can be viewed by anyone with an Internet connection; it generally provides basic details about listings but often withholds specific addresses. The private site, on the other hand, provides real estate agents with all of the available information about homes identified in a search, including the address, showing instructions, and home details.

Your MLS data sheet (see Figure 4-1) is the landing page, the place where buyers and agents must go to learn more about the details of your home. Because of this, successful sellers understand that the MLS is first and foremost a marketing vehicle for their listing, a one-stop shopping environment that will provide the vast majority of the showings of their home. Because of this, how well a home is presented in the MLS can ultimately determine the seller's success. Let's look at four ways to make sure your home stands out in a sea of competition.

Figure 4-1

1. *Multiple photos.* Most MLS systems now allow agents to place not just one but multiple photos of their listings online (see Figure 4-2). Placing a listing in the MLS system without a photo is like trying to talk someone into a blind date. It's a tough sell. But it's even harder when a buyer has the option of looking at several other

Figure 4-2

listings in his price range that include multiple photos. *Advanced tip:* Make sure you establish your preference concerning the lead or first photograph; this is important, as the first photo will often be printed and handed out to buyers in the field.

2. *Virtual tours.* Most MLS systems allow an agent or seller to link a virtual tour to a listing. A virtual tour provides buyers with the ability to walk through your home while still at their own home or at a real estate agent's office. But be careful; not all virtual tours are created equal. A true virtual tour is more than just a slide show of photos; instead, it should give buyers the freedom to explore a home room by room using "hot spots" (see Figure 4-3), offer an audio description of the home, and provide easy-to-use controls. For a great sample of a well-crafted virtual tour, check out www.visual tour.com.

Figure 4-3

Advanced tip: If you decide to use a virtual tour, be sure to include the link information not only in the MLS system but in all of your marketing materials, including flyers, signs, and websites.

3. *Remarks.* Most MLS systems provide agents with a section where they can make added remarks about a listing. While many agents look at this as simply a place to rattle off showing instructions or added amenities, wise agents look at this section of the MLS data sheet as a small but powerful advertisement. It's the place where homeowners and real estate agents need to sell the sizzle. *Advanced tip:* Ask your agent to provide you with a copy of the MLS data sheet so that you can review and approve of the content.

4. *Complete data.* Nothing will frustrate an agent or buyer faster than missing or incomplete information on an MLS data sheet. Successful sellers ensure that their listing data are complete and accurate. Small details matter. For instance, double-check:

- Driving directions to the home
- Heating and cooling sources
- School districts
- Tax and insurance information
- Showing instructions
- MLS zone (geographic listing area)

Advanced tip: Ask your agent to send over a copy of the MLS data sheet after any changes have been made to the listing.

Once you have built your MLS strategy, it's important to understand what happens to the data in your listing, because in most cases this information doesn't just sit idle in one database; instead, it is often shipped off to many different online marketing aggregators.

Aggregators—Real Estate Marketing Engines

Tonight, while you are sleeping comfortably in your king-size bed dreaming of giant marshmallows, something is happening, something important. Your listing information is probably being "scraped" out of the MLS database and dumped into one or more online databases. Although this might sound ominous, don't worry; this isn't a group of teenage thrill seekers. Instead, it is a high-tech way of selling the same product, your home, in many different online outlets. Within the real estate industry, these outlets are sometimes known as real estate aggregators.

A real estate aggregator is a company that pools real estate information and stores this information in a massive database that consumers can search online. The most successful real estate aggregator is www.REALTOR.com, which contains more than 90 percent of the single-family homes listed in the United States. Other large aggregators include www.realestate.com and www.realestate/yahoo.com. Real estate aggregators can take many forms, but the flow of information from a real estate agent or a private seller to an aggregator's website is relatively simple.

Once a home is listed for sale, either through a real estate agent or in some cases by a private seller, the information

> ### REALTOR.COM STATISTICS
>
> - REALTOR.com has over 5.5 million unique users per month
> - The average REALTOR.com visitor spends nearly 20 minutes per visit.
> - REALTOR.com has more than 90 percent of U.S. single-family listed homes, with daily updates from over 800 Multiple Listing Services from all 50 states, Canada, and Puerto Rico.
>
> *Source: MEDIA METRIX, January 2004, and Internal Logs.*

is quickly uploaded to the MLS database. This gives all the real estate agents in the community the ability to show and sell the home. From there, the listing information is then scraped, usually once a day, into even larger aggregator databases that store information from many MLS systems (see Figure 4-4).

Buyers then have many choices. They can visit an agent or broker's website like the one from www.allstaterealestate.com shown in Figure 4-5, tap directly into the public MLS system, or look at multiple MLS markets by visiting an aggregator's website. The good news for homeowners is that it doesn't matter how a buyer finds your home; it only matters that she finds it. The more websites your agent or broker can place your home on, the better. Think of it as the difference between being on the shelf of one real estate company's website and being on the shelf of hundreds or even thousands of websites.

Figure 4-4   The Real Estate Data Chain

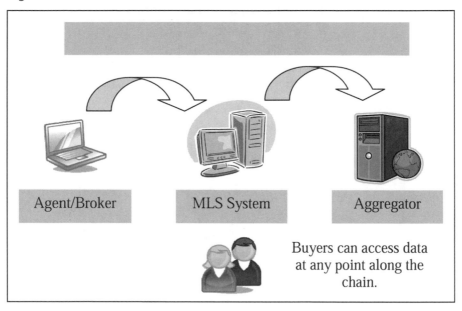

Figure 4-5

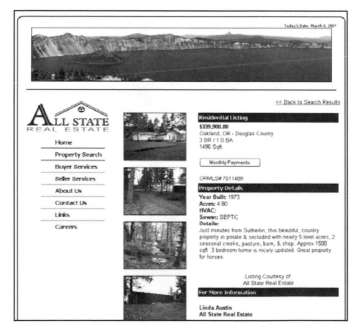

Here are some items to consider when discussing a website strategy with your agent:

Does the brokerage support IDX? Each real estate company must agree to share its listings with other real estate offices and/or aggregators in order for a listing to be shared across multiple real estate website portals. Brokerages do have the option of opting out of IDX by not allowing their listings to be shared with other companies. Of course, as a homeowner, your only concern is how you can get your home sold quickly and for top dollar. IDX technology allows you more exposure, and potentially more showings and more offers.

> **STRATEGY 26**
>
> Learn where and how your listing data are stored online.

Who receives the MLS data? As a seller, you should know all of the places on the Internet where your home can be found. In many markets, sellers must agree to allow their listings to be placed in multiple search engines. Ask your agent to provide you with a list of all the companies that tap into the MLS database.

Is the information accurate? In some instances, the process of moving data from one database to another can cause errors, as can the manipulation of listing data to fit different screen formats and templates. Be sure to double-check each aggregator's website for accuracy on a regular basis.

Is the listing enhanced? Many aggregator sites, like www.REALTOR .com, will (for a fee) allow agents to enhance their listings by adding descriptions, links, and direct contact information. In some markets, enhancements can make a huge difference in a listing's effectiveness, while in others the result is negligible.

The key to using the Internet to market your listing is to make it easy for buyers to find your home. One way in which many homeowners and real estate agents improve their odds of online success is by investing in a web page or domain specifically for their listing.

Web Pages and Domains—Making It Easy to Find Your Home Online

Assume for a second that while you're on your way to pick up some lunch, you stumble across a home that strikes your fancy. You and your main squeeze have been talking about buying a new home, and this one is just what you had in mind. Here's the rub: You would rather not pick up the phone and begin a relationship with a real estate agent quite yet. So how would you find the home online?

It's not as easy as you might think. In most cases, public real estate portals don't provide addresses on listings, so using a website like

> **STRATEGY 27**
>
> Consider purchasing a domain or web page to make it easier for buyers to find your home online.

www.REALTOR.com or the public MLS website typically won't help you find information about a specific home. You might try browsing the listing broker's website, hoping to find it there, but if you're like many buyers, you'll easily become distracted by the hundreds of other listings that can cross your online search. To solve this dilemma, many top real estate agents assign each of their listings a specific web page that can be accessed directly over the Internet. For instance, an agent may assign the address www.allstaterealestate.com/123johnson to one of his listings. This "online address" can then be added to every marketing piece or advertisement for the property, in addition to being added as a sign rider. Buyers can then quickly access property details over the Internet without necessarily having to speak with an agent.

This technique is known as creating a web page for a listing, or a page within a broker's or agent's website dedicated to a specific property, sort of like letting your brother rent a room in your house. Of course, the downside to this arrangement is that any guests of your brother have to come through your front door to get to him. Likewise, for a homeowner, the downside to a web page is that a buyer must pass through a broker's website to enter your listing page. While this may not be a big deal, it can cause a buyer to lose focus, which is why many agents and private sellers choose to invest in a domain name.

A domain name is an online address that points to a website or web page. You can purchase a domain name quickly and inexpensively at online registries like www.godaddy.com or www.networksolutions.com. For instance, if you live at 123 Johnson St., you might decide to buy www.123Johnson.com. This would give you the ability to point your new domain name to any web page or website that you choose. For instance, if your broker has a web page dedicated to your listing, you could simply point your new domain name to this web page, so that instead of having to type www.abcrealestate.com/123johnson.com, a buyer could simply type www.123johnson.com. Both addresses lead to the same place on the Internet.

Homeowners who choose not to list their home with a real estate agent can actually go one step further than just investing in a domain name. They can build a website specifically for their home. That sounds hard, right, building a website? It's actually very easy, as almost all online domain registries, including www.godaddy.com and www.networksolutions.com, will not only sell you a domain name but also sell you a template for building a website and even provide hosting services. This means that within just a couple of hours, you can create a domain name specific to your home, build a simple website, and have the website up and running for buyers to view. For example, after purchasing the domain name www.930yates.com, the sellers of this condo in Victoria, British Columbia, built a very simple website using a template generated for free at www.vflyers.com (see Figure 4-6).

Figure 4-6

*Flyer provided by Joel Burslem of the blog www.futureofrealestatemarketing.com.

Once you get your website up and running, it's time to leverage the Internet to create an explosion of interest in your home. How do you do this? Let's take a look at advertising your home online.

Advertising Your Home Online

Advertising online, like gambling online, can be both dangerous and expensive. Everyone wants to take your money, but very few offer you any real chance of earning anything back in return. For instance, sellers can easily spend thousands of dollars on banner ads and search engine placement optimization, both with the promise of increased exposure, only to end up with an empty wallet and no seafood buffet in sight.

To avoid this fate, think like a buyer. If you were shopping for a home online, where would you look? The natural first stop for many buyers will be a real estate aggregator or a large real estate search engine. If your home is listed with a real estate agent, relax; it's highly likely that your home will automatically be placed into databases like www.REALTOR.com and many others free of charge. Even private sellers can tap into the power of aggregator websites for a small fee by using databases like www.yahoo.com/realestate, www.forsaleby owner.com, or www.luxuryhomesandproperties.com.

But, of course, that's not the only place buyers will look. Local buyers, who tend to shop a little harder and dig a little deeper, might also turn to the less traveled road of online classifieds. Why? The ability to wind our way through the back alleys and dark corridors of Internet classifieds gives us the thrill of a modern-day treasure hunt. It's something we can't resist.

The largest online classified website portal in the country is www.Craigslist.com, but there are many others as well including the following:

POPULAR ONLINE CLASSIFIED SITES

www.Craigslist.com
www.Oodle.com
www.Backpage.com (powered by Oodle)
www.Local.com (powered by Oodle)
www.Lycos.com (powered by Oodle)

www.Propsmart.com
www.Edgeio.com
www.Vast.com
www.HotPads.com

One company that offers owners and agents the ability to post listings on all of these sites without having to tediously cut and paste their work is www.postlets.com. Currently free, this Web provider offers owners and agents a one-stop posting service where they can build one advertisement and then port it over to all the sites listed here quickly and easily.

STRATEGY 28

Increase your home's exposure by advertising on classified advertising boards.

But before a buyer lands on one of these classified advertising boards, he may take a short detour back to your local newspaper. Why? Many newspapers have invested tens of millions of dollars in building online versions of their newspapers that include slick, sophisticated, and, most importantly, searchable classified ad sections. You may find listing your home in your local newspaper's online classifieds to be a far more economical and effective way to market your home than traditional print advertising, and you may just find your next buyer!

Once they have selected the marketing venues that will make their home stand out, many agents and owners turn up the heat by using an advertising widget (see Figure 4-7). Widgets, which were once primarily used in social networking sites like www.myspace.com, are small scrolling windows of information that can display both text and photos. Why use a widget? Because widgets are fun. They can turn a boring text ad into a fascinating tour of your home, neighborhood, or backyard. For a complete list of widget makers and providers, visit www.widgetbox.com.

One way in which agents

Figure 4-7

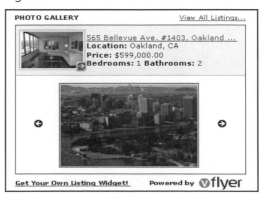

and owners can use their new widget is to market their home on one of the most successful online retailing websites in the world: www.ebay.com. Boasting hundreds of thousands of property tours a day, eBay offers something that many competing websites can't: a high traffic count. While this doesn't necessarily mean that people will look at your home, it does improve your odds dramatically. Think of it as the difference between opening a restaurant just off the freeway and opening a restaurant ten blocks away from the nearest stoplight. Which location will drive more business through your front door?

Speaking of your front door, another exciting online advertising tool that has recently been offered to the real estate industry free of charge is Google Base. Google Base is a service that makes it easier for home buyers and real estate agents to find your home when they use Google to look for properties. For instance, imagine a buyer who is looking for a three-bedroom home in Orlando, Florida. She might type in a search for "Three-bedroom home for sale in Orlando, Florida." This search, in turn, would return a map of Orlando with an overlay of all the three-bedroom listings that have been entered into the Google Base system. The best part is that it costs nothing to enter your home into the system.

Once you have mapped out your online advertising strategy, it's time to decide how you will handle an e-mail inquiry. The best Internet marketing plan in the world can still fail if you are unable to turn an anonymous e-mail into a live walking, talking buyer.

Responding to an E-mail Inquiry— Three Cut-and-Paste E-mails

Here's a typical e-mail exchange between a buyer and a seller.

Subject Line: Home/Information

Hi—I'm interested in receiving more information about your home, which I saw on a Craigslist advertisement. Can you tell me the address?

Subject Line: Home/Information

Hello—Sure. The home is located at 123 Sherry St., in Eugene, Oregon. Thanks.

Responding to this question seems pretty straightforward—just give the person what he wants, right? But pinning down an anonymous Internet buyer is like trying to catch a stray cat—difficult at best. To pry Internet buyers loose from their cozy leather recliners, you need to offer them something irresistible, something that will move them out from behind their ergonomic keyboards, into their cars, and down the road to your front door.

Fortunately, the secret to catching stray cats and elusive Internet buyers is exactly the same. First, you have to know what doesn't work. For instance, like trying to chase down a cat, sending repeated e-mails to an Internet buyer won't work. Also, attempting to sneak up on an Internet buyer, as on a cagey feline, by attempting to befriend him is a losing proposition as well. No, the best method for catching Internet buyers is to offer them some-

STRATEGY 29

Be ready to handle buyer inquiries by e-mail.

thing they can't resist: a little buyer catnip, or what we humans call real estate information.

Buyers are magnets for real estate information. What information can you offer a buyer that will make her purr like a kitten? Here are ten pieces of information that most buyers won't be able to resist:

1. *Detailed CMA.* A copy of your competitive market analysis.

2. *Utility costs.* A copy of your utility bills for the last year.

3. *Financing information* A breakdown of how a buyer can finance the property.

4. *School district information.* A report card on the local school district.

5. *Incentive plans.* A description of your selling incentives.

6. *Photos/virtual tours.* A link to more photos and/or a virtual tour.

7. *Construction details.* A description of unique construction details.

8. *Neighborhood photos.* A variety of photographs of your neighborhood.

9. *Neighborhood profile.* A profile of local stores, services, worship centers, and so on.

10. *Home history.* A brief history of the home's unique heritage (if any).

As selfish as this may seem, Internet buyers don't care about anything other than their own needs, which is exactly why building trust and rapport with an Internet buyer is such a challenge. Successful sellers look at their relationship with an Internet buyer the way a good chef looks at a meal. A good chef doesn't serve the entire meal on one huge oversized platter. Instead, she parcels out her masterpieces over the length of the entire meal, beginning with an appetizer or a starter, and progressing to another course and then another until finally the main event is served—the entrée. Likewise, successful sellers offer Internet buyers small bites of information, enough to motivate the buyer to continue the discussion, whetting his appetite for the main course—a tour of the home. Let's take a look at three sample e-mails using this technique:

E-MAIL 1: OFFER A CMA TO THE BUYER

Subject Line: Information/Home Advertisement

Thank you for your interest in our home advertisement. We've had many inquiries over the last few days.

Many buyers have enjoyed reading a copy of the Competitive Market Analysis report that we based our pricing decision on. This report includes a list of all of the homes in the neighborhood that are actively for sale, have sold, or are now pending. Just let us know and we would be happy to e-mail you a copy.

To answer your specific question: <Answer>

The home is available for showing by appointment tomorrow morning or afternoon. Which works best for you?

Thank you again for your interest. We look forward to talking with you soon.

Sally Seller

<Phone Number>

<e-mail>

Notice that in this e-mail, the seller offers additional information before answering the buyer's question. Why? Because if she answers the buyer's question first, the buyer has no reason to keep reading—

why should he? Also, this savvy seller doesn't give away the added information within the e-mail itself; instead, she offers it as a way to continue the dialogue.

Now, to be honest, many sellers might balk at handing over a competitive market analysis to a buyer, but unless your home is vastly overpriced, what's to hide? A diligent buyer or his agent is likely to discover the data within a CMA at some point anyway. Why not remove the question marks and give it to him now? But before you fire up your MS Outlook account, let's check out a couple more e-mails:

E-MAIL 2: OFFER A UTILITY COST REPORT TO THE BUYER

Subject Line: Information/Home Advertisement

Thank you for your e-mail. It's nice to have so much interest in the home.

Many buyers have asked us about the local utility costs. We actually took the time to compile our annual costs for water, sewer, garbage, power, and gas into a small report. Would you like us to e-mail you a copy?

To answer your specific question: <Answer>

If you have some time, we would be happy to give you a quick tour of the home. We are open tomorrow morning or afternoon. Which works best for you?

Thank you again for your interest. We look forward to talking with you soon.

Sally Seller

<Phone Number>

<E-mail>

Notice that this e-mail again uses the promise of valuable information as an enticement to continue the new relationship. The frame for the discussion is that other buyers have found the information to be helpful. Given this context, many buyers will feel a certain sense of competitive curiosity. They want to know what everyone else knows. They don't want to be left out of the knowledge circle. Let's look at one more e-mail:

E-MAIL 3: OFFER NEIGHBORHOOD PHOTOS

Subject Line: Information/Home Advertisement

Thank you for your e-mail. We've had several inquiries, so our ad must be working!

One thing that we keep hearing from buyers is how important the neighborhood is in making their ultimate decision. To help buyers get a sense of our community, we have put together several photos that show not only our home but also the entire neighborhood. Would you like me to e-mail you a link to the slide show?

To answer your specific question: <Answer>

If you have some time, we would be happy to give you a quick tour of the home. We are open tomorrow morning or afternoon. Which works best for you?

Thank you again for your interest. We look forward to talking with you soon.

Sally Seller

<Phone Number>

<E-mail>

Because buyers rate the quality of the neighborhood as one of the most important factors in purchasing a home, this e-mail can be incredibly effective. To take this approach one step further, you may want to create a virtual tour of the neighborhood by highlighting all of the best parts of your community.

So now that you have mastered the art of romancing a buyer, how about real estate agents?

E-mail Marketing to Real Estate Professionals

If you have hired a real estate agent to represent you in the sale of your home, it's likely that a large part of her marketing efforts will be devoted to pitching your listing to other real estate professionals. Strange, isn't it? You would think your agent would devote her time to marketing your home to buyers. But actually, that is what she's doing. Remember, it's highly likely that it will be an agent within the MLS system that will bring in the buyer who eventually purchases your home.

STRATEGY 30

Market your home to top-producing real estate agents by e-mail.

Because of this, one powerful method that agents can use to keep your listing top of mind is to use a peer-to-peer e-mail marketing campaign. This technique starts with an agent's compiling a list of the top producers in the market and then e-mailing them about your home. For instance, take a look at this sample:

E-MAIL: TOP PRODUCER E-MAIL MARKETING SAMPLE

Subject Line: New Listing—147 Smith River Ave.

Good Morning,

Just a quick note: I listed a new home at 147 Smith River Ave.—MLS #123459. The property features two streams, a 4,000-square-foot home, and access to a boat ramp. One item not listed in the MLS printout: The property next door is For Sale by Owner, so this could be a two-family setup.

Come by this Thursday for a REALTOR tour! We will be serving BBQ ribs.

See you there!

John Superstar

ABC Realty

It's important that an agent be succinct in his message and that he have a compelling reason to send an e-mail in the first place. If an agent or owner is only repeating what is already listed in the MLS system, the e-mail may simply be viewed as a nuisance or an irritant and be deleted out of hand. Also, repeated e-mails that add no new information to the listing can be viewed as desperation marketing—something to avoid at all costs. Instead, every e-mail must have a reason for being sent. Here are a few of the best reasons an agent can send an e-mail:

- New listing announcement
- Price change/terms change
- Added information
- Showing instruction changes
- Invitation to open house

For a flashy version of the same technique, many real estate agents are now outsourcing their e-mail flyers to companies like www.zipyourflyer.com that provide a full-color flyer template and a complete e-mail database of local real estate agents. For a small fee, the listing agent plugs in the listing data and photos, selects the market area, and then authorizes the flyer to be sent (see Figure 4-8).

Figure 4-8

Of course, it's not just real estate agents who can use e-mail to market a listing. Successful private sellers can also send e-mails to real estate agents. Understandably, if you choose to send out an e-mail to the real estate community, you have to accept a few things. First, real estate agents don't work for free. They will expect to be paid if they sell your home, so you need to decide up front what you will offer a selling agent as compensation. Second, real estate agents are likely to see your e-mail as an invitation to solicit your listing. Don't get mad; in fact, if you are considering hiring a real estate professional, this can be a great way to find agents who aren't afraid to ask for your business. Third, you probably will have only one shot at making an impact, so make your e-mail a good one. For instance, take a look at this example:

SUBJECT LINE: FSBO—1452 SW Grange Ave.

Good Morning,

As you are one of the top-producing real estate agents in the area, we wanted to let you know that we have decided to sell our home, located at 1452 SW Grange Ave.

The home is 1,450 square feet with three large bedrooms and two baths. We have had new carpet installed this year, and the home features oak cabinets, a walk-in pantry, and a raised garden bed. The home is also easy to show and available for immediate occupancy. For details, you can take a virtual tour by clicking on this link: Home Tour.

Currently we are selling this "For Sale by Owner," but we will cooperate with any real estate agent who would like to sell the home by paying an X% fee.

Thank you

Mr. and Mrs. Johnson

You might notice that in this e-mail, the sellers have decided to use an old-fashioned text-based e-mail, but to their credit, they have included two hyperlinks. A hyperlink is a word or phrase that is linked to more information. This technique allows the reader to open a link from your e-mail to a web page, website, virtual tour, or virtual flyer that contains more detailed information about your home.

Now that you've thought about the various ways you can market your home, including web pages, flyers, and print ads, the best way to really drum up interest is to consider giving incentives to potential buyers. Let's explore this together in Chapter 5, "Positioning—The Power of Incentives."

C H A P T E R   5

Positioning—The Power of Incentives

Incentives are an incredibly powerful sales tool, one that is used by nearly every successful company on earth to encourage buyers to take the plunge and buy its products and/or services. Why are incentives so powerful? Because they have a deadline, a drop-dead date when the increased value will evaporate and the poor sap who didn't take advantage of it will be kicking himself for not jumping in while he had the chance.

Walk through any mall and you will see a thousand so-called sales, discounts on items from kitchen towels to doggy sweaters that will expire in just a few days or hours unless you "act now" or "buy today." But hold on; if these sales are really sales, shouldn't they end at some point? You would think so, wouldn't you? But they don't. Why not? Because retailers learned decades ago that shoppers like to feel that they've beaten the system, cracked the code, and won the cold war by getting a pair of Levi's for 20 percent off the sticker price. As a result, most stores now have perpetual sales, sales that may end for a day, but, like a computer after a power outage, immediately reboot.

STRATEGY 31

To motivate buyers
to take action,
consider using sales
incentives.

In real estate, sales incentives can be a great way to motivate an otherwise reluctant buyer to get off the fence and come running like a teenager to the ring of his BlackBerry. As the real estate market has become more competitive, Ruth Simon of the *Wall Street Journal Online* has noted this trend among the nation's top builders:

> Across the country, builders are stepping up their incentive programs. Ryland Group Inc., which builds homes in 27 markets, now budgets an average of 3.7% of a home's purchase price for buyer incentives. On a $254,000 home, the builder will kick in roughly $9,400 for extras such as a "bonus" room, landscaping and window coverings. In addition Ryland is offering home buyers free flat-screen TVs in Atlanta and a choice of upgrades, including stainless-steel appliances and the first year's homeowners' association dues, in Minneapolis.

So what are some ways in which you as a seller can use sales incentives to drive up interest in your property? One way might be to red tag your home and hold a one-day-only sale.

The One-Day-Only Sale

Angie Martinson, a top-producing real estate professional from southern Oregon, has always been creative when it comes to marketing, but this time it was her assistant, Gene, who stumbled on the idea of using a "one-day-only" sale. Gene came up with the idea after watching a television commercial that ended with the famous tag line "Limited Time Offer!" Why not apply that to real estate, Gene thought, and the next morning she brought the idea to Angie.

Angie loved it; in fact, she had just the house to test the concept on. The home, located in a nice of area of town, was well kept and easy to show, but unfortunately, it just wasn't attracting enough buyers. Showings had been flat. The starting price of $219,000 had been competitive, but now the sellers were willing to adjust the price to the next major price point of $199,000. Instead, Angie made the suggestion that they try a "one-day-only sale" in the form of an open house.

To promote the event, Angie first told her coworkers and MLS colleagues, called all of her investor friends, and placed an advertisement in the local newspaper (see Figure 5-1). Next, she teamed up with another agent to handle the traffic, and she invited a local lender to help qualify buyers on the spot. Finally, on the morning of the open house, Angie and her partner canvassed the neighborhood; set up signs, balloons, and flyers; and then planted themselves at the listing.

So did it work? Absolutely. The one-day-only sale was a huge success. Angie and her co-host showed the home to 10 groups of buyers, but more importantly, two of the buyers asked to write an offer on the spot, and one of them eventually purchased the home.

Figure 5-1

1243 Johnson St – Eugene, OR
Saturday 1:00-3:00 pm

Price Reduced dramatically to $199,000 for one day only. Custom three bedroom, two bath home featuring views, maple cabinets, and hardwood floors. Don't miss this opportunity for instant equity!

Now, of course, it's impossible to say for sure what it was that finally inspired the buyers to reach for their pen, but there's no doubt that the starting point for getting people to the front door of the home was the limited-time offer, combined with a substantially lower price. This technique is a classic example of something that we in the real estate business call the fear of loss close, which simply means that people hate to lose.

So will a one-day-only sale work in your situation? It depends on the situation. In this case, the seller was prepared to make a substantial price reduction down to the next major price point. This combined with the fact that the home was in good condition and in a good location only fueled the fire of interest.

Of course, the one-day-only sale is just one type of sales incentive. Let's take a look at several more ideas.

Five Irresistible Financial Incentives to Offer Buyers

Buyers are cheap. Not because they want to be, but because they have to be. It's expensive to buy a home. It doesn't matter whether you're a first-time home buyer or you're buying an island; when you add it all up, entering into a real estate transaction is extremely expensive. For instance, Figure 5-2 estimates the market value of a median-priced house over a 30-year period. The top line represents real house prices; "real" prices are prices that have been adjusted for inflation. The bottom line represents nominal (actual) house prices. Notice that in the 25-year period from 1975 until 1999, inflation-adjusted house prices stayed roughly within the range of $120,000 to $145,000. But since the year 2000, these prices have risen significantly above the top of this range. The median price in the United States was approximately $213,000 as of year-end 2005, or 48.5 percent higher than the previous housing boom peak of an *inflation-adjusted* $143,400 in 1989.

Figure 5-2

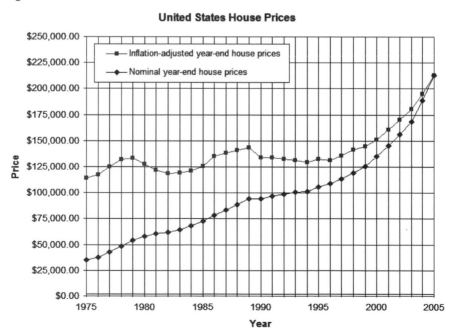

So while some homeowners sit idly, fingers crossed and lucky shirt on, and wait for the sky to start raining buyers, creative homeowners are proactive. They put their home in the best possible position to attract a buyer. How? One way is by using financial incentives. Let's take a look at the top five financial incentives you can use to attract a qualified home buyer.

The Top Five Financial Incentives to Attract a Buyer

1. *Pay the points.* Points are fees charged by lenders for providing financing. In general, 1 point equals 1 percent of the mortgage balance. For instance, a buyer paying 1½ points on a $200,000 loan will pay $3,000 in loan fees. As an incentive to write an offer, some sellers offer to pay the points on behalf of the buyer. As Elizabeth Weintraub, a full-time broker-associate at Lyon's Real Estate in Sacramento, California, points out, "As a selling expense, points reduce the amount of any gain you realize from the sale and are deductible by the buyer."

2. *Buy down the interest rate.* Many buyers are unaware that they can secure a lower interest rate by paying additional points at closing. Just like the points discussed in the previous paragraph, a point used to buy down the interest rate is 1 percent of the sales price. For example, a buyer who is securing a $300,000 mortgage and is paying 1 point in loan fees and then another 2 points to buy down her interest rate will pay a total of $9,000 in loan costs at closing. If she can save any portion of this amount by choosing one home over another, it might very well sway her decision.

3. *Pay for closing costs.* Closing costs are fees charged by escrow companies and lenders to process the paperwork necessary to close the sale. While sellers generally pay for insuring clear title by purchasing title insurance on behalf of the buyer, many homeowners decide to offer to pay the buyer's closing costs as well. If you do so, it is wise to put a cap on the amount of closing costs you are willing to pay by stating that you will pay "up to" a certain predetermined amount.

4. *Pay for inspections or compliance work.* Lenders typically require inspections before funding a buyer's loan. While in many areas of the country these are typically paid by the buyer, they are almost always negotiable. The same is true of any needed repairs that might

be revealed by inspections. To secure a sale, many sellers will offer to pay for inspections and/or compliance work "up to" a reasonable amount.

5. *Carry the contract.* For sellers who own their homes free and clear, or who have a large amount of equity, offering to provide owner financing by carrying the contract might be a viable option. Owner financing means that the seller acts as the bank by agreeing to accept payments from the buyer. The advantage to offering owner financing is that buyers can save thousands of dollars in loan fees and can often close the sale very quickly. The downside is that you take on additional risk should the buyer default at some future point. Before offering or accepting a sale with owner financing, always seek the advice of legal counsel.

If these incentives seem too big to justify, like shooting mosquitoes with an elephant gun, you might consider starting smaller, perhaps by offering the buyer a few prepaid items.

Five Prepaid Items That Buyers Love

Maybe all your buyers need is a bottle of wine, a spa treatment, or a gift basket to motivate them to take the first step on the road to buying your home. I know—give your buyers a spa treatment? But in Sonoma County, California, development company Christopherson Homes did just that when the supply of homes doubled in over a year, glutting the market. "We wanted to let outside brokers know that we were move-in ready for their clients. It was important to get their attention," said Brenda Christopherson, co-owner of the Santa Rosa–based company. "It turned out to be more successful than we ever imagined. We only expected to sell a few homes." To get brokers' and buyers' attention, the company offered drawings for just looking at its custom homes—including bottles of the luxury Silver Oak wine, Healdsburg Hotel spa treatments, and Nordstrom gift certificates.

STRATEGY 32

Prepaying for buyer conveniences can be the tipping point for buyers to move forward.

Did it work? Absolutely. The company closed 20 deals over the next month. "It works to get agents to come out and view properties.

It creates more activity," said Alice Curtis, Creative Property Services manager in Santa Rosa. "It improves your odds because it's a numbers game."

So how can you improve your odds? Offering prepaid items as an incentive to purchase a home is one way many sellers generate buzz about their homes, so let's take a look at five prepaid items that buyers love:

1. *Upgrades.* Everyone loves to be upgraded. Better seating, better food, bigger sizes, better service—yeah, upgrade me! Because of this, many builders now allocate as much as 5 percent of their sales price to sales incentives that they offer to buyers in the form of upgrades. This technique can be a great way to set their homes apart from the competition by offering kitchen and bathroom upgrades, landscaping upgrades, or even carpet upgrades to motivate buyers to take action.

UPGRADES VS. ALLOWANCES

How is an upgrade different from an allowance? An allowance is a credit given to the buyer to compensate her for accepting a home's defects, things like worn-out carpets, failing plumbing, or poor drainage. An upgrade, on the other hand, is a credit given to a buyer for areas of the home that the buyer would like to customize or personalize to suit her own tastes.

2. *Free appliances.* Many sellers are now offering to provide buyers with their choice of brand-new appliance packages, from front-load washers and dryers to new convection ovens and even plasma televisions. This incentive can be a real plus for buyers who have never owned a home before. It's also a plus for any buyer who wants new appliances, like just about everybody.

3. *Prepaid utilities.* Like getting stung by a bee once a month, adjusting to a new mortgage payment can be painful. One way sellers can swab on the calamine lotion and make it easier for a buyer is to prepay utilities for a certain period of time. This could include prepaying for gas, electricity, cable TV, or even Internet services.

4. *Prepaid services.* Owning a home isn't easy. You have to clean the darn thing, mow the grass, maintain heating and air conditioning systems, clean the pool, clean the gutters, and even change the lightbulbs once in a while. Because of this, some sellers throw in a prepaid service such as a lawn-mowing service, a pool-cleaning service, or even a housekeeping service to encourage buyers to step up and write an offer.

5. *Vacations.* Buying a home is one of the most stressful events in a person's life. After managing the thousand little details it takes to move in, unpack, and get settled into a new home, most buyers are exhausted. So it's a great time for a vacation. But how can buyers afford one? They can if the vacation was thrown in as a perk for buying the home, something that many sellers and builders are doing to spur activity. For example, in the Bay Area, Pulte Homes San Francisco has given buyers a vacation for two in either Hawaii or New York.

There is no doubt that providing buyers with prepaid items is a great way to set your home apart, and the more valuable the perk, the more likely it will be to attract a buyer's attention. Vince Brennan, a Realtor with Re/Max New Trend in Farmington Hills, Michigan, reports that his clients have even agreed to prepay for a year of property taxes just to push buyers over the edge.

Of course, with sellers becoming more and more aggressive in their tactics, it's easy for the offers to become more and more lavish. But is there a limit?

Cars, Cash, and Craziness

The downside to using selling incentives is that buyers can easily become like spoiled Oscar nominees who care more about their Gucci gift bags than about their golden statues. Because of this, some aggressive buyers have been known to demand that sellers provide cash back at closing, new cars, or more.

For sellers who are considering using incentives, this can be a dangerous position to be in. Do you give in and give the buyer what he wants just to get the house sold, or do you stand firm and tell him to take a walk? One big consideration in this decision should be the legal implications of providing an incentive to a buyer. For instance, is it even legal to give something to a person in order to motivate him to purchase your home?

The short answer to this question is yes, it is legal, just as it's legal for the makeup salesperson at Nordstrom's to give you a free bottle of mascara if you buy the hottest new wrinkle treatment. Incentives, like taxes, are a part of the capitalist machine; they won't soon leave us. Now for the long answer, which is: It depends. The biggest consideration is: Is there a lender involved in the transaction?

A lender is a party to the sale agreement. No, the lender isn't the buyer or the seller, but there's a small detail here: The lender is the one with the money. No money, no deal. Before it provides financing, a lender looks at two big things. First, it looks at the buyer. Does she have good credit, a good job, and a good history of paying her debts? Second, it looks at the home. How much is it worth? What is its condition? What is the lender's risk? If the risk is relatively low, or at least acceptably low, it will fork over the bananas to the buyer, and you, the seller, can run off to Tahiti.

Now here's the problem. Suppose you as a buyer come to me and say something like, "Listen, I'll buy your home, but I need you to buy me a new car." And I start by saying, that's obscene, offensive, and nuts, but finally I say, "Okay, what color would you like?" We now need to tell our friend the lender about this.

Why is it the lender's business?

Because the lender's assumption is going to be that in order to pay for this new car, either I, the seller, will have to inflate the price to cover the cost of the car, or you, the buyer, will have to pay my already high price in order to make the deal happen. In either case, from the lender's standpoint, the home is worth exactly what the buyer paid, after subtracting the cost of the new car, cash, or any other incentive the seller provides.

Why do lenders look at it that way? The reason is that if the buyer defaults on the loan and the lender has to take the home back, the home will have to be resold. If it is not worth what the buyer actually paid for it, the lender will have to take an even bigger loss, since the car, cash, or other incentive is probably already long gone. Because of this, a lender will want to be sure that if a home sale includes an incentive, the home's equity can still cover the lender's risk.

To make this all clear, selling incentives are legal; they can be and are used by sellers across the country, but they must be disclosed to the buyer's lender. This full disclosure is absolutely mandatory. A buyer may argue and say, "It doesn't really involve you, Mr. and Mrs. Seller. It's my lender." But that won't matter if the lender believes that you willingly participated in fraud. Fraud? Yes; if you provided a new car, cash, or some other incentive to the buyer without telling the lender, it could be looked at as bank fraud. Don't do it. Fully disclose all selling incentives to the lender in writing.

Now, before you get too scared of using selling incentives and run for cover in the next chapter, let's take a look at one of the least expensive, most effective selling incentives that every seller should use (and that lenders love).

Why a Home Warranty Is a Win/Win

Today everyone wants to sell you a warranty. So it's no wonder that when I talk to sellers about a home warranty, their first reaction is to grab their wallet.

To be honest, the first time I heard about home warranties was in the early 1990s. My wife and I had purchased our first home in the same month we were due to deliver our first son. It was early August, hotter than the hubs of hell, and as I switched on the air-conditioning unit one morning, it kicked over like an old Buick and then sputtered to a halt. As I picked up the phone to call a repairman, it suddenly dawned on me that the seller of the home had included a home warranty in the sale. Skeptical as I was, I was also eager to save a few bucks, so I dialed the 800 number and mentally prepared for the worst. To my surprise, the friendly voice on the other end of the line told me that a repairman would call me that same morning and make an appointment to diagnose the problem.

By mid-afternoon we had the culprit, a blown compressor unit. The bad news: It would take a week to get the part, and the unit would cost $1,200 installed. The good news: The home warranty company agreed to pick up the tab minus our $100 deductible. The only trouble with this solution was that my very pregnant wife couldn't stand the heat for another week. After we explained our dilemma to the home warranty company, it put us into a hotel for the duration. Three days later, the compressor was fixed and we were back home. So now I'm a convert; I think home warranties are the greatest thing since water beds, and I think every one of my clients should use one.

But let's start at the beginning. What is a home warranty, anyway?

A home warranty is a service contract that helps protect against the expense of repairing or replacing covered home appliances and mechanical systems that break down as a result of normal wear and tear. This can be expensive; just check out the statistics compiled by HMS Home Warranty Company on the average cost of home repairs (see Table 5-1).

TABLE 5-1

System/Appliance	Repair/Replacement Cost
Furnace	$1,250–$3,500
Air conditioning	$700–$3,275
Oven or range	$700–$1,225
Refrigerator	$600–$900
Dishwasher	$500–$700
Washer or dryer	$200–$500
Water heater	$375–$425
Broken water pipe	$100–$600

Suppose you're a buyer who is looking at two homes; both of them are similarly priced and they have roughly the same amenities, but one seller is offering you a free home warranty that protects you for up to one year for covered mechanical system breakdowns, and the other isn't. Which one would you choose? You guessed it—buyers love home warranties. Just check out these statistics:

STRATEGY 33

Consider using a home warranty with the sale.

Benefits of a Home Warranty*

1. *Warranted homes sell faster.* Warranted homes sell up to 50 percent faster than unwarranted homes.

---

*Based on a National Home Warranty Association report and Gallup Poll statistics.

2. *Warranted homes sell at a higher price.* Warranted homes are perceived as a safer investment and on average have a selling price of up to 3 percent more than their competitors without a warranty.

3. *Warranted homes are preferred.* Eight out of ten buyers prefer to buy a warranted home.

4. *Reduced chance of a delayed closing.* With home warranty protection, the chance of conflict over a malfunctioning system or appliance is minimized.

Now how much will a home warranty cost? Costs vary by state, but in most cases a home warranty will cost a seller between $300 and $500, depending on the coverage limits. Every home warranty contract includes a list of standard coverage items and a list of options. For instance, optional items might include coverage of the roof, pool heaters, or hot tubs. Of course, these options come with a fee attached, so when you begin shopping for a home warranty, be sure to compare all of the plans available in your area. To make it easy, most home warranty companies have a website where you can compare their rates and the features of their programs; for instance, Warrentech (*www.warrentechadvantage.com*) provides a state-by-state contact list of local warranty specialists who can provide you with an instant quote by phone.

Now let me give you the big closer on home warranties, the reason that every smart seller should immediately offer a warranty on his home today. Ready? A home warranty doesn't cost you a nickel unless your home actually sells. That's right, you pay for it only at closing. Where's the downside? There is none. But that's not all; to make their products even more attractive to sellers, home warranty companies often offer sellers free limited coverage during the listing period.

Okay, you're sold on a home warranty; what else can you do to motivate the market to beat a path to your front door? One secret that successful homeowners have been using for years is to offer selling incentives to real estate agents.

Selling Incentives for Real Estate Agents

In most states, real estate agents representing a buyer have a fiduciary responsibility to show their client every home that is on the market, regardless of the size of the commission being offered. But human nature being what it is, ask yourself, if you were a real estate agent with a list of ten homes to show, nine with sellers offering you a 2.5 percent commission and one with a seller offering you a 3.0 percent commission, which home would you show first? The one with the bigger commission, right? Of

STRATEGY 34

To motivate real estate agents, provide a selling incentive.

course, as an ethical and responsible real estate agent, you would be required to show your client all of the homes, as well as disclose the amount of your compensation, including any sales incentives, but the truth is, most buyers probably couldn't care less about how much you're being paid as long as they can purchase the property at a fair price.

The key to this technique is increased showings. For example, if your home averages one showing a week when you offer a typical commission, in most markets this means that it will take you nine to ten weeks to locate a buyer, as on average home buyers look at nine homes before making a buying decision. By offering an increased selling agent commission, you may be able to dramatically increase the number of showings per week, thus decreasing the time it takes to secure an offer.

But is it really worth it to pay the selling agent a higher commission?

To be honest, it depends on the market conditions and your own motivation to sell. For many of my clients, this technique has been the key to selling for top dollar in their own time frame. Because of this, I encourage sellers to think of themselves as sales managers. As a sales manager, your job is to motivate the salespeople to sell a product, namely, your home. According to a recent study, one of the best ways to motivate any sales force is to reward the members of that sales force with an incentive. Check out these numbers:

• 81 percent of North American executives run sales incentive programs to increase or maintain sales.

- 27 percent of salespeople recorded significant productivity increases when provided with a sales incentive.
- 92 percent of salespeople stated that sales incentives were the number one reason why they achieved their sales goals.

The bottom line for any seller is that increased commissions, like any selling incentive, need to be looked at in the context of the entire transaction: Will they help you to accomplish your end game?

It's important to note that selling incentives can also have strings attached. For instance, according to a report from the *Wall Street Journal Online*, Las Vegas builder American West has offered agents as much as a $15,000 bonus to sell homes in its Glen Eagles development, provided they come in with a full-price offer within 30 days. But the bonus drops to $10,000 for negotiated offers and those that take longer. Jeff Canarelli, vice president of sales, explains, "The goal is to try to push them to make a full-price offer."

In offering your own selling incentives, you too can put limits on how and when you will provide a bonus. For instance, you could determine that a bonus will be paid only if you receive a full-price offer or an offer within a certain time frame. Of course, to motivate any agent, these targets have to be realistic. One of the biggest mistakes that agents and sellers often make is to attempt to bribe an agent past the price. All sales incentives are a waste of time if the home is overpriced. It's like trying to sell a rotten salad to a vegetarian. No matter how much salad dressing you offer him, he's still going to want the tofu burger.

Selling incentives for real estate professionals can take many forms. Let's look at four creative strategies for supercharging your sales force.

Four Ways to Supercharge Your Sales Force

1. *Increase the fee.* As already mentioned, you might offer to pay the selling agent more money in the form of an increased percentage. But you might also consider increasing the listing agent's fee. Either way, both agents will be more motivated to place your home at the top of their priority list. (You might even increase both.)

2. *Offer cash.* The downside to just offering the selling or listing agent a higher commission is that the agent will probably have to split the money with her broker. To help avoid this, some sellers agree to pay a cash bonus to the selling agent at closing, in addition to

the agreed-upon fee. Since the broker is still participating in the original agreed-upon commission, the entire cash bonus is often handed over to the agent (with the broker's approval).

3. *Offer a vacation.* Another way for sellers to motivate salespeople is to offer them a vacation should they sell the property. Many successful homeowners offer a choice of destinations payable only when the home has successfully closed. *Quick tip:* Don't book the trip until the home sells, since many agents will prefer the cash equivalent.

4. *Offer a lavish gift.* Obviously a bottle of wine probably won't be enough to motivate a salesperson to show your home, but a bottle of wine with tickets to a sought-after local event, say a concert or a sporting event, might just do the trick. One key to success when offering gifts is uniqueness. The more the idea is unique, the higher the chance of its gaining an agent's attention.

The fastest, easiest, and cheapest way to motivate your listing agent is the promise of more business. Why? Your listing agent is always hungry for more real estate deals; this is why we often train new agents to look at a listing as the opportunity to create not one but two transactions. The first is the sale of the home, and the second is helping that same seller buy her next home. By engaging your listing agent in the search for your next home, you will dramatically increase the agent's motivation to sell your current residence. Why? Because he will see not one but two commission checks on the horizon, something he can't resist (see Figure 5-3).

Figure 5-3 One Agent—Two Possible Transactions

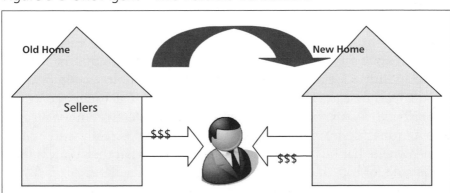

But believe it or not, the money train doesn't stop there. Some savvy agents are actually able to create three transaction "sides" from a listing.

Three Sides to the Story: Representation and Motivation

Something that is important but that is often forgotten when you list your home with a real estate agent is the possibility that your listing agent may end up becoming the selling agent as well. This means that, depending on your state laws and the real estate company's internal policies, your agent could end up representing both sides of the trans-action, both the seller and the buyer. What does that mean? From a commission standpoint, it means that a real estate agent is likely to double her income if she sells the listing herself, as she will earn both the listing commission and the selling commission.

Some sellers are shocked by the idea that an agent can represent both sides of a real estate transaction, something that they see as akin to an attorney representing both sides in a divorce. Obviously, this is something that you need to discuss in depth with your listing agent should you decide to work with a real estate professional. But setting aside the legal issues, from an agent's standpoint, being able to "dou-ble-end" a transaction is like getting to eat dessert twice: a rare treat.

When an agent is allowed to work on both sides of the transaction, this can be a huge motivator. Of course, he has to do twice the work, both the selling agent's job and the listing agent's job, to earn this fee, but being able to work on both sides of the fence gives agents a much better chance of actually closing the transaction. Why? Because there is one less person to communicate information through, one less obstacle in a negotiation, and one less person to make mistakes.

Of course there are some sellers, and even some real estate brokers, who argue that real estate agents shouldn't be entitled to earn a fee on both sides of a transaction; more importantly, they shouldn't be allowed to represent both sides of a real estate transaction. It's a complicated debate. Of course, there is an easy fix to the issue: Real estate agents can just sell one of your competitors' homes and completely remove the rep-resentation issue from the table. But is that what you really want? Most homeowners that I talk to don't really want that; what they want is their home sold for top dollar.

Figure 5-4 One Agent—Three Possible Commissions

Of course, if you do choose to allow your agent to represent both sides of the transaction, she gets an added bonus, because she now has the opportunity to earn three separate commission checks. How? First, she will be paid as your listing agent; second, she has the opportunity to sell the home and be paid as the selling agent; and third, she has the opportunity to sell you your next home (see Figure 5-4).

Now before steam starts coming out of your ears, consider that when you sell a home and buy a new one, all of these fees will probably be paid to someone. It's really only a question of who will receive the fees: Will it be one highly motivated agent, or will it be three slightly less motivated agents?

To be fair, the odds of your listing agent actually being the agent who sells your home are not as high as you might imagine. While the listing agent's job is to market the home, what often happens is that the marketing spurs buyers to contact their own agents, who find the property in the Multiple Listing System (MLS). These agents then show the property and bring in an offer.

Now that agents and other potential buyers are interested, you should be thinking about how you'll prepare your house for open houses and showings. Let's dive head first into these waters in Chapter 6, "Preparing Your Home for Showings."

C H A P T E R   6

Preparing Your Home for Showings

Most home buyers don't expect your home to be the Taj Mahal, although they do demand that their next castle be the best that their money can buy. This means that within their price range, home buyers will shop for a home that gives them the most value per dollar spent. Because of this, they don't look at your home the way you do; they look it as a house, one of many houses that they will see, and when your home is just a house, it's really just a product.

To sell your house and turn it back into a home, you have to position your product to offer the most value per dollar spent. You have to sell it. To do this, many successful sellers have learned that regardless of how good their home looks on the inside, it won't matter if a buyer can't get past the outside.

A great example of this is a 2006 study of home buyers and sellers conducted by the National Association of Realtors, where it was found that buyers rated neighborhood quality as the number one factor in purchasing a home. So what if your neighborhood leaves a little (or a lot) to be desired? Check out this quick list of ideas compiled by Trish, a Realtor from Mississippi, on helping to clean up a neighborhood.

Cleaning Up the Neighborhood

Strike a deal. If your neighbor's home is dragging your listing down, why not spring for a landscaper to give his yard a makeover? Why pay for a neighbor's yard to be improved? So that you can sell your home for top dollar.

Call the city or chamber of commerce. Ask if there are any neighborhood cleanup programs available. Many volunteer organizations pick an area each month to clean or improve. Why not your neighborhood?

Team up. If there are other homeowners in the neighborhood who are attempting to sell their homes, why not team up to tackle the problem? A combined effort over one weekend—picking up trash, cleaning out storm drains, or painting over graffiti—could inspire others to follow your lead.

Of course even the best neighborhood might not be enough to win over a buyer's interest if your home itself doesn't make a good first impression. This is exactly why successful sellers make a point of focusing on improving their home's curb appeal.

Curb Appeal—Ten Ways to Make a Better First Impression

Home buyers look at homes the way college students on an Internet dating service look at potential dates: quickly and ruthlessly. They don't care what a home looks like on the inside unless it looks good on the outside. The good news is that you can improve your home's curb appeal dramatically by spending as little as a weekend preparing the home for sale. How? Let's take a look at 10 ways to improve your home's curb appeal.

1. *Paint the home.* Painting your home is one of the best ways to improve its curb appeal, and if you do it yourself, it can be relatively inexpensive. Architectural expert Jackie Craven agrees: "A well-chosen selection of contrasting trim and accent colors can draw attention to architectural details and disguise design flaws."

2. *Paint the trim and the front door.* A home's front door is the gateway to the home. Make sure that it is clean; if needed, consider a quick coat of paint. Painting a home's trim can also be an easy way to make the home seem more appealing.

3. *Plant flowers.* There is no better way to brighten up a front yard than to plant flowers. According to landscape expert David Beaulieu, "Perennial flowers are wonderful for your planting beds, but they bloom for only so long. You may have perennials blooming in your bed in May, then nothing until July. Incorporating annuals into a do-it-yourself landscaping plan will 'plug the gaps,' giving you continuous color in the yard."

4. *Clean the downspouts and gutters.* A home may have a beautiful paint job, but if the downspouts and gutters are in need of a good washing, repair, or even replacement, this can make the whole home seem less desirable. For many homeowners, this can be quickly solved with a bucket, an extension pole, and a couple of good washrags.

5. *Clean the screens and windows.* Most buyers never take the time to think about windows or screens unless they are dirty. If they are, watch out, because buyers will then start scrutinizing other areas of a home's exterior for flaws. Don't give them the opportunity.

6. *Pressure wash the sidewalk and driveway.* Like a good facial, pressure washing a sidewalk or a driveway can take years of grime, dirt, and age off of your home's exterior.

7. *Keep it green.* While mowing the grass would seem like a given, edging, fertilizing, and keeping the grass watered and weeded is something that many homeowners should take the time to do, as the yard is one of the first things many potential buyers will see.

8. *Replace outside light bulbs.* Because many buyers will drive by your home during the evening, it's important to make sure that your home shows well at night. A well-lit home can seem warm and inviting, while a poorly lit home may seem dark and scary.

Quick Tip: To light up your real estate "For Sale" sign at night, check out using a solid-state, battery-operated LED lighting system like the one from CyberLux (www.cyberlux.com).

9. *Clean, paint, or replace house numbers.* When buyers and agents are searching for your home, they will be looking for your house number. Because of this, you want to be sure that your numbers are easy to find, clean, and inviting.

10. *Remove all cobwebs and spray for pests.* When removing cobwebs, give special attention to the areas under the eaves and around lighting fixtures, windows, and roof lines. If your home has never been sprayed for pests, this may be a good time to have a professional spray it.

Items an Inspector May Review

Sure, as a homeowner, you may be under no obligation to go looking for problems with your home, but in most states you do have an obligation to disclose any known material defects. This means that if you don't disclose a problem that you know of—a leaking sewer line, for instance— you could end up paying for it even after closing, plus the cost of attorney's fees and any other remedy a judge might decide to levy.

Prudent sellers will tell buyers everything they know about their home, good or bad, but this begs the question, what if there is something hidden, something that you don't even know about? Obviously, you can't disclose what you don't know, which is why most buyers, on the advice of their real estate agent, request an inspection prior to closing.

So what will the inspector be inspecting? It depends on the type of inspection being conducted, but buyers are often encouraged to conduct a whole house inspection, or an inspection from the foundation to the ceiling, top to bottom, inside and out. In that case, the inspector is likely to be looking at a list of items that would include the following:

Doors, Stairs, and Walkways

- All doorways, stairs, and walkways are free of obstructions and solid.
- All stepping-stones should be firm.
- Railings should be steady.
- Check external doors for good weather stripping and thresholds.
- Doors are level and easy to open and close, with good hardware.

Drainage

- Downspouts drain away from the house.
- Yard slopes away from the house to draw water away.
- Earth is at least six to eight inches below the top of the concrete foundation.
- Gutters are well attached and in good condition.
- Crawl space, if any, has a vapor barrier (heavy-gauge plastic).

Roof

- Check for leaks or conditions that might lead to leaks.
- Make sure no trees are touching or overhanging the roof.
- Look for dry rot or other problems around overhangs.
- Check the condition of the shingles.
- Find out the age of the existing roof.

Windows

- Check for dry rot around panes and in sills and frames.
- Check for cracks in glass.
- Make sure windows open properly.
- Check caulking and seals on windows.
- Check for moisture damage inside.
- Check that windows are large enough to escape through in case of fire.
- Check casement windows to see if the hardware is working properly.
- See whether double-hung windows have broken sash cords.

Fireplace

- Check for crumbling mortar around brickwork.
- Look at stability of chimney.
- Check for obstructions.

- Make sure flue is lined with terra cotta (brick is in violation of most codes).
- Check to see if there is a working damper in the fireplace.

Floors

- Check the condition of the floors or carpet, testing for soft spots in floor.
- Check for moisture damage to parquet floors.
- Check for water damage, especially around plumbing fixtures and under floorboards and supports.

Foundation

- Check for cracks, shifting, or settling.
- See if house is bolted to foundation (earthquake safety).
- Make sure mudsill is in good condition and dry.
- Check whether foundation has been retrofitted.
- Look for structural problems like cracks in the basement floor.

Heating and Cooling

- Make sure the furnace thermostat is operational.
- Check the furnace venting.
- Find out the ages of the heating and cooling equipment.
- Run both the furnace and the air conditioning to check output.
- Check insulation—attic, walls, and floors.

Improvements

- Has there been remodeling or improvements to the house?
- Check the licensure and credentials of the builder, owner, or technician.

Miscellaneous

- Check that kitchen appliances and faucet are operational.
- Check for asbestos, radon gas, and lead.

- Check for cracking or peeling paint.
- Check attic ventilation.

Pests

- Look for termite and beetle holes in wooden supports and under house.
- Check attic vents for hornet or wasp nests.
- Check for rodent droppings in cupboards and under house.
- Look for chew holes in roof, eaves, and wiring from squirrels and other rodents.

Plumbing

- Check for leaks around pipes and fixtures.
- Test water pressure (turn on more than one faucet at a time).
- Test hot water pressure (same method) and check if there's enough hot water.
- Check walls around shower for water damage.
- Look for rust or leaking around hot water heater.
- Make sure water heater is up to code.
- Find out the age of the water heater.
- Ask whether the hot water system has been updated in any way.

Walls and Ceiling

- Check the condition of drywall walls and ceilings.
- Pay particular attention to the condition of taped joints.
- Look for waves or cracks in the walls or ceilings.
- Look for water spots from leaks in the roof.
- Look for settlement cracks in walls.

Wiring Systems

- Check for blown fuses, overloaded circuits, broken outlets, or flickering lights.

- Test outlets, light sockets, and switches to ensure that they work properly.
- Check to see if the system has been updated—three-prong outlets, circuit breakers, and so on.
- Look for GFI (ground fault interrupt) outlets in bathrooms and kitchen.
- Look for broken or loose outlets.
- Test light fixtures.

Some sellers want to remove all the surprises from their home sale. These anxious homeowners often hire an inspector to do what is referred to as a pre-inspection. A pre-inspection is just what it sounds like: an inspection before the buyer's inspection.

By doing a pre-inspection, a seller can find out her home's hidden flaws and has the chance to fix them before putting her home on the market. For some, this can alleviate some of the nail-biting stress that waiting for a buyer's inspection report can induce. But there is a potential downside: If your pre-inspection reveals any problems, it's likely that these flaws will have to be disclosed to a buyer. Of course, if you planned to fix the problems anyway, this is no big deal (unless one of the problems revealed is so monumental that it can't be fixed). But if you don't have unlimited resources, this may be something to consider carefully.

So now that your home, the product, has been completely flight-checked and is ready for takeoff, what else can you do to improve your odds of success? Let's explore this together in Chapter 7, "Showing Your Home to Potential Buyers."

C H A P T E R   7

Showing Your Home to Potential Buyers

Buyers notice cleanliness. A clean home is something that they can smell, feel, and touch; it's both tangible and intangible. Unfortunately, what with a full-time career, kids, and trying to cook dinner every night, housework comes in a distant second on the priority list of most homeowners. Of course, now that you're selling your home, you might want to keep in mind the old joke from the military that goes: "If it moves, salute it. If it doesn't move, pick it up. If you can't pick it up, paint it."

For deep cleaning, sometimes known as spring-cleaning, you start by moving all of your stuff, like knickknacks, toys, bookcases, lamps, and furniture, and cleaning underneath it. Nothing is too heavy, too big, or too cumbersome to move. From the highest point in every room down to the baseboards and floors, everything gets cleaned.

> **STRATEGY 35**
>
> Deep cleaning your home can help you sell your home faster and for top dollar.

Making a home shine is hard work, but the payoff can be huge, as your home will be in a much better position to impress a buyer. So let's take a look at a list of ideas for making your home sparkle.

Ideas for Making Your Home Sparkle

Basic Deep Cleaning Tips

- Make your every move count. Get organized before you start.

- Focus on the job at hand. Distractions will drag out the job.

- Put all your cleaning supplies in a tote so that you can carry them with you.

- Begin at the back of your home and work your way to the front, cleaning from left to right, back to front, and top to bottom for maximum efficiency.

- Try to clean regularly. It's easier to do routine cleaning.

Kitchen Cleaning

- Vacuum, mop, and wax wood floors.

- Vacuum and then mop linoleum or vinyl floors.

- Wash and clean baseboards.

- Clean inside and outside the refrigerator.

- Change the shelf liners.

- Clean out the junk drawer.

- Wipe the inside and outside of the cabinets.

Bathroom Cleaning

- Dust and wash the windows.

- Clean window tracks and window screens.

- Clean the toilet, shower, and sinks.

Window Cleaning

- Vacuum or dust draperies.

- Wash or dry-clean blinds.

- Clean windows, screens, and window tracks.

Furniture Cleaning

- Polish wood furniture.

- Vacuum cloth upholstery. Clean and condition leather upholstery.

- Vacuum under and in between cushions.

- Clean under couches, chairs, and beds

Closet Cleaning

• Donate clothing that you no longer use to charity.

• Vacuum floors.

• Dust walls and shelves.

• Place cedar blocks in the closet to freshen up the air and prevent moths.

Cleaning Baseboards

• Grab a clean, absorbent rag and dampen it in a soapy solution, wringing it as dry as possible. Start at one end of the baseboard and wipe all the way along the top and the sides around the perimeter of the room.

• Go over the baseboards again with a used fabric softener tissue from your dryer. This will help prevent dust from settling on the baseboard.

Floor Cleaning

• Sprinkle baking soda on your carpets to absorb stale or musty odors.

• Buy floor mats for every entrance. They help reduce tracked-in dirt.

For an exhaustive list of ideas sellers can use to prepare their home for sale, check out www.housekeepingchannel.com.

Once you have your home shipshape and ready for inspection by even the pickiest buyer, it may be a good time to consider removing showing distractions.

Removing Showing Distractions

Are you a collector? Do you collect clocks, spoons, plates, model trains, or bicycle tires? If so, you may want to recognize that these collections take up space and can make even a large home seem small or crowded. Also, because these items are so unique to your tastes, they may actually make it more difficult for a buyer to bond with your home.

For serious collectors, packing their treasures before the home is actually sold gives them an opportunity to spend more time and

STRATEGY 36

To help buyers visualize themselves living in the home, pack up your collections.

attention ensuring that their valuables are properly preserved. Some items to consider packing:

- Dishes or china that are rarely used
- Small appliances that are not used often
- Clothes that are not in season
- Unused linens, towels, and covers
- Furniture that crowds any room
- Exercise equipment that is not in use
- Collections or antiques
- Books and/or videotapes
- Magazine collections
- Toys that are not being used

Packing up your favorite personal items may be hard to do, but it is the first step toward helping buyers visualize themselves living in your home. To help them even more, many sellers use a creative technique known as home staging.

Staging Your Home—Helping Your Home Tell a Story

Home staging is a selling tool used by successful sellers around the country to enhance their home's best features. Home staging simply means that a home is like a stage on which a story is being told. The better the story your home can tell, the better your chances of creating excitement and interest in your home will be.

According to Ellen Boettcher, president of Staging by Design, real estate professionals advising homeowners should assess several factors when listing a home for sale, the first of which is: How bad is the place? "Maybe the general appearance of the property is dated, worn, or unattractive," says Boettcher. For this reason, many real estate agents recommend utilizing the services of a professional home stager or, if they have been trained to provide these services themselves, offer their own staging recommendations. What will they recommend? Let's look at nine expert home staging ideas:

Expert Home Staging Ideas

1. *Think clean and open spaces for your home as you stage.* Don't be afraid to let in the light and clear out the dust.

2. *Take a tour of your home.* Pretend that you've never seen the house before, and give it a critical look. Get picky. Make a list of things you'd like to improve.

3. *Remove all personal items and photographs.* Removing all possible barriers a buyer may have to making a connection with your home is a great way to increase the chances of a sale. Home buyers have an easier time envisioning themselves in your home if your personal items are removed.

4. *Clear off all surfaces and keep only a few decorative accessories.* For example, in your bathroom and kitchen areas, bring in some new towels and finish off the look with a vase of freshly cut flowers or candles.

5. *Think of ways to clean, eliminate clutter, and modernize.* "When in doubt," one expert advises, "pack it out. You'll be happy to have your home packed up when it sells faster than expected."

6. *Eliminate odors from smoking, pets, and cooking.* In one study, 53 percent of buyers said that strong odors such as pet or cigarette smells had a bigger impact on their impression of a home than the overall tidiness and cleanliness.

7. *Let the home buyers see all the rooms.*

8. *Clean your carpets and touch up the paint.*

9. *Clean your exteriors.* Sweep and dust the front entrance. Put out a new doormat, and clear away cobwebs and dust. Landscaping should be cleared of dead brush and overgrown plants.

As a homeowner, you might want to follow the advice of Peggy Selinger-Eaton, author of *The Art of Staging*: "You don't need to be a decorator to stage a home. Check out leading department and home furnishing stores to see what colors they are using and copy them. Bringing in trendy colors immediately modernizes any home, as will fresh linens in the bedroom and bathroom."

So what is a trendy color, anyway? Good question. To find the answer, let's take a look at choosing the right room colors.

Color Me Sold!—Choosing the Right Room Colors

One of the biggest ways to influence a buyer's first impression of the interior of your home is by choosing the right room colors. Researcher Debbie Zimmer of paint manufacturer Rohm & Haas says that there is a psychology of color that sellers can use to help make a good impression on buyers:

- *Red*. The color red can increase blood pressure, heartbeat, and energy in most people. It instills feelings of intimacy and passion, and increases the appetite. Red is often a good choice for a formal dining room.
- *Orange*. Orange works well in living rooms and family rooms because it can warm up a room in a friendly way. Sellers often experiment with various tints and shades to find the best match for their tastes.
- *Yellow*. This color is warm and welcoming, but it is more of an attention getter than either red or orange. Because of this, it is often a good color for poorly lit foyers or dark hallways.
- *Blue*. This color makes most people feel tranquil and at ease, which makes it ideal for bedrooms. Blue has also been shown to be an appetite suppressant, so it is not a good option for a dining room.
- *Green*. This is a relaxing color that many find more versatile than blue. Light greens are ideal for bedrooms and living rooms; mid-tones are good for kitchens and dining rooms.
- *Violet*. Many adults dislike purples, but are fond of the rose family, which can work in many rooms. Young children, on the other hand, seem to like violet, so this color can be used successfully in children's bedrooms and play areas.

Now, nobody move. The home is clean and ready for showing! Sometimes it's easy to feel like you need to move to a hotel after you've deep-cleaned your home because you don't want to go through the pain and suffering of cleaning it again if it gets dirty. Not to worry; once your home has been deep cleaned, preparing for a showing should be a matter of a light touch-up.

The 20/20 Rule of Preparing Your Home for a Showing

Buyers always seem to want to see your home at the wrong time. Like right before dinner or when you need to take your kids to day care. Sure, you could tell them to take a short walk off a tall building, but that won't get your house sold. Instead, successful sellers use the 20/20 rule, meaning that with a little planning and a lot of hard work, they can have their home ready to show in 20 minutes using a simple 20-point checklist. How do they do it?

First, they rally the troops. This is a team effort; everyone has to pitch in. To motivate younger players, you might offer them a small bribe in exchange for their help. Second, savvy sellers have already done the deep cleaning recommended earlier in the chapter, so the home shouldn't need a complete overhaul. Finally, they have a system, so that they know exactly what needs to be done and who will be doing it when the alarm sounds.

> **STRATEGY 38**
>
> Put together a home-showing plan for your family.

So are you ready to turn on the stopwatch? Let's start!

20 Last-Minute Things to Do Just Before a Showing

1. *Mini mop-ups.* Sweep the kitchen, bathroom, and entry. If needed, use a cleaning towel or sponge to remove any spots or debris.

2. *Dust the furniture.* A quick wipedown of the furniture, TV screens, and computer monitors can help make each room shine.

3. *Clean off counters.* All counters should be clear.

4. *Beds made.* All the beds in the home should be made.

5. *Garbage cans empty.* All garbage cans need to be empty.

6. *Carpets vacuumed.* Give the carpets a quick once-over to fluff them up. Focus your efforts on the entry and living room.

7. *Lights on.* A dark home is gloomy. Turn on all the lights in the home, and open drapes and blinds to brighten the home.

8. *Load the dishwasher.* Clear the dishes out of the sink and off the counters by loading the dishwasher.

9. *Load the washer.* Clothes should be picked up and either placed in a hamper or loaded into the washer.

10. *Pick up every room.* Work backward from the entry point of the home to the furthest bedroom.

11. *Turn on soft music.* Think relaxing instrumental music that will put buyers at ease as they walk through a home.

12. *Set the temperature.* The home should be at a comfortable temperature; for most buyers, this means between 68 and 72 degrees.

13. *Freshen it up.* Try placing a drop of vanilla on a lightbulb in each room of the house, or simply light a candle to add an inviting smell to your home.

14. *Clean out the entry.* Remove shoes, toys, and garden supplies from the front entry. This area should be clean and inviting.

15. *Pick up the front yard.* Sprinklers, bikes, basketballs, and other miscellaneous items should be put inside the garage.

16. *Extra vehicles.* If you have extra cars or trucks, consider moving them down the street so that the home's exterior doesn't look cramped.

17. *Open all rooms.* Buyers want to see the entire house. A closed or locked door can be a huge turn-off.

18. *Turn on fireplace.* If you have a gas fireplace, this is a great time to light the fire.

19. *Display photos.* Do you have photos of the home during different seasons? Show them off!

20. *Display flyers.* Place your home flyers on the kitchen counter, along with any additional information you may feel is relevant.

Wow! That's a big laundry list to get through in only 20 minutes. But just think: If your efforts result in a great showing or perhaps even an offer, won't that little bit of elbow grease be worth it? Of course! June, a real estate broker from northern California, agrees: "Buyers who have seen nine or ten homes in one day see it all . . . dirty homes, unkempt homes, barking pets, screaming kids . . . so they really appreciate it when a seller has prepared their home for a showing. It does make a huge difference."

As big as the 20/20 list is, there are two important items that are not on the list that can make or break a showing. What are they? The first is what to do with your pets during a showing.

Pets

What do you do with your pets during a showing? I know what you're going to say because I hear the same sentiments from pet-loving sellers every day:

> "Our dog would never bite anyone; she'll just lick you to death."
>
> "We've never even heard him bark."
>
> "You won't even know she's there."

Of course I believe you, but let me paint you a picture. Imagine a couple who has just arrived at your home. They're all smiles; they've taken a virtual tour of your property, driven by the home seven times in the last three days, and even been prequalified for a loan. They can't wait to see the inside! But as soon as they ring the doorbell, they hear something. It's the deep baritone of approaching death. Like one of the four horsemen of the apocalypse, your friendly pet has been transformed into a monster. As your once-friendly pooch claws at the front door, howling and growling with greedy anticipation of what will be next on his dinner menu, what do you think has happened to this couple's excitement level?

Of course, it's not just dogs that can be an issue. Cats can pose an especially tough challenge. For example, here's something that I've seen on many listing data sheets: "PLEASE DON'T LET CAT OUT!" As a real estate agent, once I read this, I know two things: First, the one and only mission in this poor cat's life is to get out, and second, I'm going to spend my entire showing focused not on selling the home, but on making sure that the darn cat doesn't get out!

> **STRATEGY 39**
>
> Decide in advance how you will handle your pets during a showing.

Ah, but I have exotic pets—pets that are in cages and don't bark or try to escape, like birds, snakes, spiders, lizards, rats, mice, hamsters, or even guinea pigs (I've seen all of those in homes for sale). Those should be okay, right? Well, it depends. If you are selling your home to people (or parents) who have seen a few exotic pets, it might not be an issue. But if you happen to attract someone who has arachnophobia, a fear of spiders, or musophobia, a fear of mice, it could very well cost you a sale.

To deal with the issue of pets of all makes and models, follow these simple rules:

Pet Rules for Home Showings

1. *Ideally, remove all pets during showings.* In a perfect world, all pets should be removed from the home during showings. This eliminates any chance that a pet can be a distraction. To help with this, try asking a neighbor or family member to become your favorite creature's adoptive parents during showings.

2. *Contain the pet during showings.* The second-best choice is to use a pet carrier or utility room to confine the pet to one area of the home during showings.

3. *Name the pets.* If your home is listed with a real estate professional, make sure that the pet's name is listed on the MLS data sheet. With this information, the agent can calm the pet's nerves (and her own) by calling the pet by name while showing the home.

4. *Cover the pet areas.* For exotic pets or pets that may frighten a potential buyer, cover the cage so that the buyer doesn't come face to face with his worst fear. (Just make sure you don't create a fire hazard.)

5. *Make the pet disappear.* Make sure that your home is free of pet smells by having the carpets thoroughly cleaned, pet areas washed, bedding replaced, and old pet toys disposed of. Also because many people have allergies to pet dander, try using an air purifier with a HEPA filter or change your home's built-in air filter system to a high-grade HEPA filter once a week. Also remember to vacuum the home thoroughly before each showing.

So now that your pets are taken care of, what about you? Should you, the seller, be present during the showing of your home? It's an excellent question, and one of the most important considerations when showing your home.

Should You Stay or Should You Go?

Go! If your home is listed with a real estate agent, there is absolutely no question that leaving the home during a showing improves your odds of success. Why? With the homeowner gone, buyers tend to ask more questions, open up drawers and closets, peek behind bathroom shower curtains, study the floor plan, measure rooms, and mentally move in. This is exactly what we need them to do. We want buyers to buy into the home, to visualize themselves already living in it. To do this, buyers need space; they need room to think.

> **STRATEGY 40**
>
> If possible, always leave the home during a showing.

Yet like someone who pays a mechanic to fix his car but then grabs a wrench and crawls under the hood, many homeowners insist on being present during a showing. Helpless, real estate agents are forced to bite their tongues as they watch sellers point out things that a buyer could care less about while not even mentioning the features of the home that the buyer has already indicated are critically important to her. In the end, the showing is blown.

The advantage that a real estate agent has over a homeowner during a showing isn't that he knows more about the home than the homeowner does; it's that he knows more about the buyer. For instance, he knows what the buyer is looking for, what the buyer likes and dislikes, and ultimately what will motivate the buyer to write an offer and hire a mover. So take a walk, go out to dinner, or go grocery shopping, but do something—anything—to get out of the house during a showing!

Okay, we get it, but what if we stay in the house but don't say a word?

With a homeowner sitting quietly in the corner, buyers will feel like an intruder and feel pressured to move through the house quickly. No matter how many times you say, "Make yourself at home" or "Take your time," buyers will still feel awkward. Because of this, they won't really look at the house; they'll just move through it. Sure, they'll go through the motions, but they won't take the time or make the effort to build any kind of emotional connection with the house.

Trust me, real estate agents appreciate sellers who make it easy to sell their property by hitting the bricks during a showing. Of course, this can be a little bit of a challenge if you're selling the home by owner.

Showing the Home as a For Sale by Owner

If you are selling your home as a For Sale by Owner, you are acting as your own real estate agent, so you are in effect paying yourself to show the home. So guess what? Forget everything you just read: Put on your real estate agent hat and follow these simple steps to SHOW and sell your own home.

S: Set them free.

H: Hear their needs.

O: Open up to questions.

W: Work with them.

S: Set Them Free

Buyers know their own hot buttons; they know what they like in a home. For some it might be the kitchen, while for others it may be the master bathroom. Because of this, many successful homeowners follow the advice of John, a top-producing real estate agent from Nebraska: "I tell my buyers, listen, I'll give you the broad strokes about the place, then I'll follow you and answer any questions that you might have about the home." Many homeowners have discovered that giving buyers room to explore the home on their own terms makes them feel more at ease and comfortable during a showing.

RISK MANAGEMENT—WARNING

While most buyers are as honest as the day is long, some aren't. Thieves often target homes for sale, and while one distracts a seller, the other prowls the home in search of valuables. To avoid this, you might begin the home tour by saying, "Listen, if you don't mind, I would prefer that we stay together as a group. Thank you."

H: Hear Their Needs

The best real estate agents have the unique ability to tune into their clients' needs by listening carefully. Successful homeowners can model this approach by carefully asking questions and listening to the buyers' responses. Here are some questions that you may choose to ask during a showing:

- What are you looking for in a home?
- What is the most important part of a home for you?
- What would you like to see?
- What attracted you to the home?

O: Open Up to Questions

Rather than just asking questions and listening to the answers, savvy sellers turn the tables and encourage buyers to ask questions themselves. By opening themselves up to examination, these successful sellers give buyers the confidence to explore lingering questions that might otherwise cause them to hesitate to take the next step. This openness can often mean the difference between a buyer leaving a home scratching his head in confusion or daydreaming about the possibilities of adding a new bedroom. To help your buyers feel comfortable about asking questions, try using this script:

> *Listen, while you're here today, I want you to feel free to ask me any questions about the home that are important to you. I know that when I bought the home, I had lots of questions.*

You might follow up this script by inviting the buyer to call or e-mail you after the showing if any additional questions surface over the next several days.

W: Work With Them

As the showing winds down, many private sellers feel somewhat lost. They don't know how to take the next step, or, as we say in the sales world, "ask for the order." So, unfortunately, they often just let the buyer saddle up and ride off into the sunset. This is a huge mistake because as soon as a buyer leaves your home, the chances of her coming back drop dramatically. Instead, successful sellers take a different approach by giving buyers a gentle nudge toward negotiations. How? They offer to work with buyers by throwing them a few easy pitches. For instance, they may ask one of these questions after the showing has been completed:

- Would you like to sit down and have some coffee and talk about the home?
- We have a financing worksheet; would you like to take a look?
- We have a copy of the recent sales in the neighborhood; would you like to review them?

While it's never easy to negotiate directly with someone, it can be done, if you as a seller accept the fact that not every buyer is "the buyer." In fact, most buyers won't pan out; like the tide, they will wash in and out, day in, day out, until unexpectedly one wave brings in the whale, the buyer who actually is ready, willing, and able to move forward. But before that buyer washes ashore, it's wise to anticipate just what questions a buyer may have before she commits herself to a new 30-year mortgage.

Anticipate Questions: Ten Things Every Buyer Will Want to Know

As the buyer makes his way through the dining room, down the hall, and into the bedrooms and bathrooms of your home, he will inevitably come up with questions. This isn't a bad thing. Questions are good. They show that the buyer is interested, engaged, and thinking. For a seller, the worst kind of showing is one in which the buyer silently glides through the home and leaves with nothing more than a quick glance and a polite "thank you."

You want the buyer to be thinking, debating, and struggling with the idea of purchasing your home. The more questions he asks, the more interest it shows. But what is more important than the questions that a buyer asks is the answers that you as the seller provide. A bad answer to a buyer's question can kill the buyer's interest.

Just read what a few sellers have told me as I've toured their homes:

"We would stay here, but the home is way too cramped."

"We're ready to move to a more modern home."

"It was a good place to start, but now we're ready to move up."

"The house is nice, but we don't like the neighborhood."

While giving these answers to your real estate agent may be fine, making statements like these to a buyer could cause you to lose a sale. Like any good salesperson, a wise seller thinks long and hard about how she will answer common buyer questions, concerns, or objections.

> **STRATEGY 41**
>
> Formulate answers to common buyer questions in advance.

So how can you possibly know what a buyer will ask before he even arrives at your home? You won't know exactly, but you can make an educated guess based on what most buyers ask when they tour homes. Take a look at this list of 10 things every buyer will want to know:

Ten Things Every Buyer Will Want to Know

1. *Why are you selling?* Is it any of the buyer's business why you're selling? Absolutely not. But I can guarantee you that the buyer will still want to know. So when you answer the question, just make sure you spin the reason as a positive and not a negative. For example, instead of saying, "The home is like living inside a postage stamp; it's way too small," you might say, "We're moving to be closer to work." While both statements are true, the latter statement will be far less likely to turn off the buyer.

2. *When was the house built?* Be sure to tell your buyers not just the home's age, but also the dates of recent updates or remodelings. For instance, you might say, "The home was originally built in 1955, but when we bought the home seven years ago we did a complete remodel. Let me show you what features we added."

Because many buyers perceive an older home as a potential money pit, some sellers find it wise to invest in minor home improvement projects. Many sellers replace their cabinet hardware with updated styles. The same is true of lighting fixtures and even plumbing fixtures. For bigger projects, sellers have been known to replace windows, front doors, appliances, and even garage doors to update a home's appearance.

ANTICIPATING BUYER CONCERNS

When considering the purchase of a vintage home, many home buyers understandably will want to know more about the home's systems. Wise sellers are prepared to answer questions on everything from plumbing to insulation and wiring. Remember, anything left unknown for a buyer is a black hole, something that she fears and will do almost anything to avoid.

---

3. *How old is the roof?* As a rule of thumb, a roof needs to be expected to last for three to five more years to pass most lenders' standards. So if your home has an older roof, you may want to hire a roofing contractor to do an inspection or complete repairs before you begin marketing the home. Once you have done that, you can then explain to a buyer, "The roof is years old, but we have had a recent roof inspection that shows that the roof should last at least another three to five years. Let me show you a copy."

4. *How long have you owned the home?* Buyers are often curious about how long you have owned the home. If the time period is unusually short (like less than two years), be prepared to explain why you feel the need to make a move so soon. For instance, a seller might say, "We've been here about 14 months, but our son was just accepted to college, and we want to be closer to him."

5. *How did you arrive at the price?* If a buyer begins talking about the price of the home, this is often an excellent indicator that she is interested in moving forward with a purchase. An excellent response to this inquiry might be, "We based the price on homes that recently sold in the neighborhood. I have a copy of the analysis we used to come up with the price; would you like to take a look?"

6. *How is the neighborhood?* Buyers want to know that they are moving into a neighborhood that reflects their lifestyle. Take note of the buyers you are dealing with and craft your answers around their needs. For instance, you might discover that they have kids, or that they are retired, or that they are a working couple. In any of these cases, you can adapt your answer to their needs.

7. *What are they asking for the home across the street?* If a buyer sees that one of your neighbors has listed her home for sale, it's a good bet that he will want to know the asking price of that home. Sellers prepare for this question by researching all of the homes for sale in the neighborhood along with the reasons why their home is superior. Once they have collected this information, they can answer these buyer questions with confidence. For instance, a seller might say, "They're asking $394,000, but their home has only three bedrooms and a much smaller backyard."

8. *What will you take for the home?* This is a classic buying sign: a buyer who begins fishing for more information about the price and your willingness to negotiate. Sellers who are unprepared for this question may inadvertently blurt out their lowest acceptable price and thus cost themselves thousands of dollars. A prepared seller, though, might approach the question with a question: "Well, let me ask you: Have you already been prequalified for a loan?" After receiving the answer, a seller might then follow up the question with, "May I ask what are you qualified to spend?"

9. *When can you be out of the home?* Like a family that prepares an escape route for an emergency, successful sellers need to have a contingency plan for vacating their home quickly. For instance, a seller who is having a home built may find it wise to locate temporary housing in the event that her present home sells more quickly than she anticipated. A prepared seller can then respond to this question by asking, "When would you like to be moved in?"

10. *Is the X, Y, or Z included in the sale?* Successful sellers decide in advance what items they will include and what they will exclude from the sale of their home. The challenge comes when a buyer falls in love with something that you plan to exclude. To avoid an uncomfortable conversation, consider removing any items that you plan to take with you when you leave the home. An antique

chandelier, for instance, might be replaced with a less expensive modern light fixture.

By anticipating buyers' questions in advance, successful sellers are able to create a more relaxed showing environment, an environment in which buyers can feel comfortable asking any question that pops into their head without the fear of the seller turning red-faced or becoming emotional. To expand this list, you might consider what questions cross your mind as you begin the search for replacement housing. What would you like to know about the home or the seller's situation that would influence your decision? The answers just might be the key to unlocking your own home sale.

Now before you hang up your showing hat, why not employ an approach that many top-producing real estate agents have used for years? It's a technique that guarantees that all of your buyers' questions will be answered, even the ones they forgot to ask.

Building a Home Book

There is a way to hand off your best ideas to the selling agent without even being present during the showing. How? By building a home book.

STRATEGY 42

Use a home book to highlight your home's best benefits and features.

A home book is a binder of information that includes lots of nifty details about the home that a buyer or a selling agent may find interesting and helpful during a showing. Most home books are displayed in a prominent area, like the kitchen counter, so that the selling agent will be sure to take advantage of the information. (Some owners even provide extra copies for buyers to take with them after a showing.)

To build your own home book, take a look at this list of possible information that a buyer or agent may find useful:

Home Book Sample List of Contents

- MLS data sheet
- Color flyer
- School district information

- Neighborhood description and history
- Homeowner Association information
- Neighborhood services list—shopping, worship, medical, and other resources
- Survey map of the property
- Tax assessor information
- Zoning information
- Recent inspections: roof, pest and dry rot, whole house
- Aerial map—try county services or www.google.com/earth
- Demographic information—www.uscensus.gov
- Home floor plan
- Utility bills—averages for last 12 months
- Warranties on appliances or construction
- Photographs of home—remodeling projects
- Photographs of home—different seasons
- Disclosure statement—state and federal requirements
- Offer forms—standard offer forms

The last two items, disclosure statements and offer forms, might be something you would expect to come later, perhaps during the negotiation or when writing an offer. But if a buyer gets excited about the home, why wait? By giving the agent or the buyer the tools to make an offer immediately, you have paved the way for success in selling your home.

To complement your home book, you may choose to also use feature cards. Feature cards are freestanding cards that point out special features of the home. For instance, a seller may use feature cards to point out special flooring, cabinetry, or appliance packages. As the home buyer tours the home, he can then simply look for feature cards in each room as a way to explore your home's best amenities.

Of course, home books and feature cards do no good unless the home is being shown. So how can you increase the number of showings that your home receives? One tried-and-true technique is tapping into the power of holding an open house.

Open Houses—Overcoming the 1 Percent Barrier

If you were to interview any group of real estate agents, you might be surprised to find that many of them view holding open houses as a chore, something that they do to appease sellers, but otherwise loathe. In fact, many real estate agents might confess that the odds of selling your home through an open house hover somewhere around 1 to 5 percent. Of course, this doesn't mean that real estate agents hesitate to do open houses. According to the 2006 National Association of Realtors *Profile of Home Buyers and Sellers*, 56 percent of all sellers report that their agents conducted an open house during their listing agreement, and 47 percent of all buyers report attending an open house while searching for their new home. The trouble is that when buyers were then asked where they found the home they eventually purchased, open houses didn't even register as a category.

> 56 percent of sellers report that their agent conducted an open house during their listing period.
>
> NAR, *2006 Profile of Home Buyers and Sellers*

So should you do an open house? Absolutely! An open house can be a successful event even if it doesn't directly sell your home. First, an

open house creates a unique marketing opportunity that in many cases can indirectly cause a sale to occur; second, someone who attends the open house and doesn't purchase the home may tell friends and relatives about the home, and they might know someone who will purchase it; third, preparing for an open house forces a family to keep its home in show-ready condition; and finally, as long as you adhere to some top producer guidelines for hosting the perfect open house, you may just beat the odds and sell the home. So tape up your knuckles and put on the boxing gloves; it's time to come out of your corner swinging for a knockout. Let's look at three steps for creating a perfect open house.

Step 1: Market the Open House

You know what's terrible? It's when no one bothers to show up at your open house. To avoid this scenario, follow the advice of Brian, a super-star agent from Portland, Oregon: "I start advertising my open house a week ahead of time. This gives the entire community a whole week to think about attending my open house. The longer they wait, the more curious they get!"

Brian's technique is an excellent way to build excitement about your home. To put his plan into motion, you may decide to install pre–open house signs. A pre–open house sign says something to the effect of, "Open Sunday 1–4" or "Open Sunday 12–2." By placing this sign in your lawn a week before the open house,

> **OPEN SUNDAY 1–4**

you will benefit from all of the traffic during the week, not just on Sunday.

In building your open house advertisement, pictures are obviously extremely important, as is the ad copy, but don't forget the importance of accurate directions (see Figure 7-1). A buyer who can't find your home is a missed opportunity. To create accurate directions, try using an online mapping service like www.mapquest.com. Also consider including your phone number or an e-mail address with a message that says, "Can't make the open house? Call or e-mail for a private showing." This gives buyers who simply can't make the open house the ability to come by and see the home.

In the week leading up to the open house, you may use the strategy that Shelly, an agent from Seattle, Washington, uses: "I canvass the neighborhood and hand out flyers inviting the neighbors and any of their friends and family to stop by and see the home. I've sold many homes by using this technique." In the commercial real estate world, this technique is known as rooftopping your listing. The odds are good that one of

Figure 7-1

Sea Shells by the Sea Shore

321 Ellen, Watertown
Sunday 1-4 PM

Live the dream, in this vintage Cape Cod style home. Enjoy panoramic bay views, a chefs kitchen, and loft style office. Watch the next storm cuddled up next to your own fireplace!

Directions: I-5 take exit 136, left on central, one mile left on Fort McKay, ½ mile right on Ellen.

Can't Make the Open House? Call for a private showing 555-1212

these homeowners will know at least one person who is in the market to buy a home—maybe your home!

Another especially good twist on this strategy is to specifically invite all of the homeowners who have their homes listed for sale as well as For Sale by Owners. I know: *Why do that? Aren't they my competition?* Yes and no. Sure, if your homes are similar, a buyer will probably view both of them before making a buying decision, but the reality is that she will do that anyway. By inviting competing sellers, you may be able to create a friendly partnership agreement; for instance, if a buyer doesn't like your home for one reason or another, why not refer him to your neighbor and vice versa? Another way to leverage this idea is to agree to hold a joint open house. Imagine: not just one, but two, three, four, or even five open houses available for a buyer to see over a weekend!

> **STRATEGY 43**
>
> Increase your open house attendance by modeling successful homeowners.

On the day of the open house, signage will be critically important. Most sellers will need a minimum of three to four open house signs. The main sign, of course, will be placed in front of the house itself; the other signs will be used as directional signs pointing the way to your home from side streets. Be sure to cover every possible path to your home. Some sellers and agents even add balloons to their signs to help them stand out.

Step 2: Show the Home

As you see the first buyer pull into your driveway, many questions will pop into your mind. Some may seem silly, like: Should I open the door, wait for the buyers to knock, or meet them on the porch? Others are tougher, like: What should I say as we walk through the home? This is the kitchen, this is the dining room, and this is the hallway? That doesn't seem right, does it? You might also wonder what happens if another couple arrives before the first one leaves. Do I stop in mid-sentence and move on to the next buyers?

If your home is listed by a real estate agent, relax; all you have to do is go see a movie. Let the agent worry about the details. On the other hand, if you are a private seller, have a clean shirt ready because you're going to be sweating bullets over the next couple of hours. Don't worry, that's not a bad thing; it just means that today you're working for a living.

As the first buyer arrives at your home, open the front door before she knocks and welcome her inside. Many buyers feel uncomfortable about walking into a stranger's home, so opening the door for them is often a huge relief. After a brief introduction, you may invite the buyers to sign a guest book.

A guest book like the one from www.realestatesuper center.com pictured in Figure 7-2 is a simple sign-in roster for open house attendees. Many sellers like to use a guest book because it's an easy way to collect valuable contact information about each prospective buyer. A secret trick to make buyers feel more at ease when signing your guest book is to make sure that they aren't the first to sign in. You may want to fill in the first entry with a fictitious buyer's name and contact information.

Obviously, asking a buyer you met only seconds before to kindly remove his filthy shoes can be uncomfortable. To avoid this predicament, you may want to invest in shoe booties (see Figure 7-3). Shoe booties, available at almost any

PERSONAL SAFETY TIPS

Unfortunately, hosting an open house or even showing your home can be an invitation to some to engage in criminal activity. To protect yourself and your family, follow these personal safety tips.

- Never conduct an open house or a showing alone. Always have a friend or family member with you.
- Make sure your cell phone is freshly charged. Keep it handy.
- Make sure all exits are clear and all doors are unlocked. You need to have an escape route in the event of an emergency.
- Use a sign-in registry. Some sellers require buyers to show identification at the door.

Figure 7-2

Figure 7-3

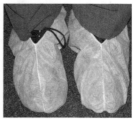

medical supply store, are protective covers that slip over shoes. Builders and real estate agents often use them for open houses and home tours.

At this point, it's time to begin the grand tour, and here, as at a fork in the path to paradise, you have two choices: You can either choose to lead or choose to be led. If you choose to lead buyers, you will maintain control of the conversation and the tour, but you can also become a potential distraction, a roadblock to the buyers being able to fully explore the home on their own terms. On the other hand, if you allow yourself to be led, the buyer in effect will become her own tour guide, focusing her inspection on the areas of the home that interest her the most, her own personal hot spots. As the buyers roam freely, you will then be available to answer questions and point out special features that aren't readily obvious. For example, check out this sample script:

> ## SAMPLE OPEN HOUSE TOUR CONVERSATION
>
> *I'm going to let you lead the way. As we go, I can point out a few special features. Where would you like to start?*

Wow, it's complex, right? No, it's just that simple. John, a top-producing real estate agent from Orlando, Florida, agrees: "When you're showing a home or doing an open house, the worst thing you can do is talk yourself out of the sale. Either the home will click with the buyers or it won't. No amount of talking is going to change that, and it might just hurt." Of course, this doesn't mean that you leave buyers to wander aimlessly through the home. For safety reasons, it is almost always best to keep a close eye on every buyer who tours your home. As the showing progresses, you may want to build rapport and trust with the buyer by asking him open-ended questions like:

- Where do you live now?
- Do you own a home now?
- Why are you considering a move?
- Have you looked at many homes today?
- When are you planning on making a move?

Many buyers are naturally reserved when meeting a seller for the first time. A seller who is able to ask open-ended questions often helps buyers to loosen up, relax, and feel at home. Of course, there is another reason to ask these questions: They can reveal a buyer's motivation or readiness to move forward. This is a critical thing to determine, especially at a busy open house, which brings us to our next challenge: What happens when another group of buyers arrives, but you haven't yet finished with the first group?

Unlike the sappy sitcom star who has booked a dinner with two dates in the same restaurant and is frantically searching for a way out of the mess, this is something that you actually want to have happen; in fact, it's a great problem to have. It means that your open house is going well, and, believe it or not, it's not as big a hurdle as you might imagine. Obviously, if you have another adult family member with you, you can simply play a zone defense and hand the buyers off to each other. But if you're playing this gig solo, you have to make some quick decisions, which is why asking those earlier open-ended questions is so important. They allow you to prioritize your attention. For example, if the buyers in the first group have yet to sell their home, their ability to complete a purchase is low. In this case, if another group of buyers arrives, you might politely say, "I just need to step away and greet the folks who just arrived, I'm going to let you continue looking at the home, and if you have any questions, don't hesitate to ask." (However, see the sidebar "Personal Safety Tips.") This then frees you to begin working with the new arrivals. On the other hand, if the first buyers are showing strong buying signals, seem ready to move forward, and have already sold their home, you might instead say, "I'm just going to step away for one moment to introduce myself to the folks that just arrived and hand them a flyer, and then I'll be right back."

Of course, because of safety concerns, it's wise never to leave a buyer unattended in your home, which is why having a showing partner is so important. But what if you don't have anyone to help you? One technique used by successful sellers and veteran real estate agents is to post a sign on the front door that says: "Showing in Progress—I'll be right with you." Another option is to take several groups of buyers through your home at the same time. Typically most buyers will spend less than 10 minutes in a home before hoisting anchor and sailing on to a different port. Because of this, in most cases you will be able to easily speak with and assist every buyer who attends your open house. Of course, you don't just want to act as a maître d'; you actually want to sell your home. This is why Step 3 is so vital.

Step 3: Follow Up With Interested Buyers

Typically, when the sparks fly, it's almost impossible for buyers to hide their excitement about a home that strikes their fancy. Like kids on their way to Disneyland, they melt into a gooey bowl of smiles and giggles. But not all buyers show their excitement in the same way. Let's take a quick look at the top nine buyer signals.

Nine Key Buyer Signals

1. *Nervousness*. If your clients begin to fidget, need to use the bathroom, or start jumping up and down, it may mean that they like the house. Encourage them to look at every detail, take their time, and ask questions.

2. *A bad poker face*. Did you ever play poker with a 10-year-old? You always know what she is holding. Hidden smiles can mean that she is holding a full house. Make eye contact with prospects and give them a big grin. They'll now be helpless!

3. *Placing the furniture*. When buyers start pacing off the bedroom and visualizing the couch, lava lamp, and end tables, it may mean that they are ready to write an offer. Keep a measuring tape or, better yet, a sonic tape handy for the buyers to borrow.

4. *Lingering*. If you have a buyer who doesn't want to leave, you have a buyer who wants to buy the house. Some real estate agents even write the offer right at the house. Wow!

5. *Running the house down*. If a buyer feels the need to run the house down, this is a clear indication that in fact he wants to talk himself out of something. Reverse the dilemma by joining him. You will be surprised at how he may then begin to sell you on the house.

6. *Asking about the price*. "What was the price again?" Oops, they just gave you a clear buying signal. If you want to have some fun, you

might say, "Before I tell you, based on what we have seen so far, what would be your guess?"

7. *Asking about why you are selling.* This often means that they are now considering writing an offer on the home, or at least that it is definitely in the running.

8. *Telling secrets.* Buyers who have an interest in a home may begin to whisper to each other. This is terrific! Give them some space and you may sell them the place.

9. *Argument.* Some couples interact only through argument. It's sad but true. If a couple begins to argue about the house, do not try to mediate the argument. This is often their way of discussing the home prior to writing the offer. Excuse yourself and let them hash it out in private.

So assuming that you have a buyer who is on the threshold of making an offer, how do you move her off the fence? First, forget the idea that you will be able to talk her into anything. Today's sophisticated buyers won't be sold or "closed." This being said, you can still encourage a buyer to make an offer by simply making it easy for her to do so. For instance, you might say:

> **"If you would like to talk about the home in a little more depth, we would be happy to meet with you after the open house is over. What time is convenient for you?"**

or

> **"We had our lender work up several scenarios for buyers to look at; if you have a minute, I can show you what she came up with."**

or

> **"Would you like to see a copy of a sample real estate agreement we had prepared?"**

I know that last one sounds a little scary, but remember, buyers who want to buy a home are on an emotional high. Like a skier at the top of a mountain, they're ready to go; all they need to do is point their toes in the right direction and go. For first-time buyers, this can obviously be a little nerve-racking, but experienced buyers can't wait to get going. They're ready to write an offer.

But what if your buyers aren't quite there yet? Yes, they're excited, and yes, they have the down payment to make it happen, but they're just not quite ready to make the commitment. What then? Do you kick them out to the curb and say, "Next"? No, you don't have to be quite that harsh. After all, these people could still end up buying the home. Instead, you need to have a good follow-up plan in place, and not just for them but for everyone who attended your open house. One way to do this is by capturing each guest's e-mail address in your guest book.

To encourage buyers to not only sign the guest book but provide their e-mail address, some real estate agents and homeowners offer drawings. A little goes a long way when it comes to open house drawings. For instance, you could give away a bottle of wine, a trip to a spa, or even just some movie tickets. Will you capture every single buyer's e-mail address? Not a chance. Will you get some bogus e-mail addresses like ABC@abc.com? Yep. But by and large, most of the e-mail addresses will be legit. A well-created follow-up e-mail will do two things: First, it will continue the dialogue with each buyer, and second, it may help you reposition your listing. Take a look at how this sample e-mail accomplishes both of these goals.

SUBJECT LINE: 123 Strawberry Lane—Open House

Thank you for attending our open house today. We enjoyed visiting with you, and we hope you enjoyed touring our home. We will be conducting the drawing for the <prize> tomorrow afternoon and will e-mail you the results.

If you have time we would value your answers to this quick survey:

1. What attracted you to the open house?
2. Did the home meet your expectations?
3. Can we answer any questions about the home for you?

Thank you again. Have a terrific day.
Suzy and Sam Seller

Some sellers may resist doing this kind of follow-up by saying, "This seems forward or aggressive." Not for a real estate agent; this is the kind of follow-up they do every day to ensure that their listings get sold, and really, when you think about it, what's the alternative? To do nothing or just wait for the next open house? In the real world, you sometimes have to shake the low-hanging fruit loose, which means acting like a salesperson.

In the end, how quickly you sell your home boils down to motivation. If you are highly motivated to sell, you will do just about anything to get the home closed. Unfortunately, some sellers, often through no fault of their own, get backed into a corner and become desperate to sell. What then? Let's find out in Chapter 8, "Extremely Motivated Sellers—When You Have to Sell Now!"

CHAPTER 8

Extremely Motivated Sellers— When You Have to Sell Now!

In the United States, 1.2 million foreclosure filings were reported during 2006, or 1 for every 92 households—a 42 percent increase from the previous year. Why so many? The culprits are often things like the loss of a job, a medical problem, a divorce, or a death in the family. Another possibility is adjustable-rate mortgages. According to the mortgage bankers association, in 2007 and 2008 as much as $1.5 trillion in adjustable-rate mortgages are due to have their interest rates raised. An increased interest rate combined with quickly rising property taxes can easily push a family over the brink. According to debt strategists at Lehman Brothers Holdings Inc., mortgage defaults may climb to $225 billion in 2007 and 2008, compared with about $40 billion annually in 2005 and 2006.

So let's assume for the sake of argument that you know someone who needs to sell fast—not you, of course; just a friend. He's in trouble, and if he doesn't sell now, he may lose his home. What are his options? The first step is to determine just how bad a situation he is in, because there's bad, and then there's "I'm seriously considering robbing a bank" bad.

Don't Panic—It May Not Be as Bad as You Think

"We're about ready to lose our house to the bank."

Sellers have told me this countless times over the years, but only rarely do any of these panicked sellers actually end up losing their home. Why? The truth is, the bank doesn't want your home. Sure, it'll take your home eventually, but only as an absolute last resort. First it'll give you plenty of time to either make up the back payments, refinance, or if necessary sell the home. To understand the foreclosure process, let's rewind the clock a bit and start at the beginning—the day you bought your home.

When you purchased your lovely abode, you probably didn't pay cash. Instead, like 92 percent of buyers surveyed by the National Association of Realtors in 2006, you either secured a bank loan or had the seller carry back a note. In either case, the home was no doubt pledged as collateral for repayment of the loan. In other words, you signed an agreement, a mortgage, that states that if you stop making payments, the bank has the right to sell the property at a public foreclosure auction.

So what exactly is a foreclosure? A foreclosure is a legal action that a lender may take to force a homeowner to make up her missed payments or risk losing her pride and joy. The process starts with a default notice, which is sent by mail to the homeowner. The default notice is a detailed history of the missed mortgage payments and the grand total necessary to bring the loan current. This amount is called the *reinstatement figure*, or the amount required by the bank to stop the foreclosure. The default notice usually says something to the effect of, Hey, make your payments, or we'll take your house. A good way to think of a default notice is as a warning shot over your bow that's designed to scare the stuffing out of you. It usually works, because this is the point when I generally get a phone call. The agitated homeowner will call in a panic and explain that he is losing his house in foreclosure and he needs to sell it by next Friday.

Of course, the truth is, the situation usually isn't quite so dire. In most cases, these terrified homeowners actually still have a significant amount of time before the actual foreclosure will take place. This doesn't mean that the wheels of commerce stop; the foreclosure process, like the marching of ants, continues slowly but relentlessly forward. If you fail to respond to the bank's default notice (usually not just one but several), the next step is for the bank to hire an attorney. The attorney's job is to advertise the upcoming foreclosure auction in the local newspaper and to file the necessary court documents. Finally, after a few more weeks (or in some cases months), the property will be auctioned to the highest bidder by the bank's attorney. The good news is that at any time up until the day of the auction, a borrower can reinstate his loan by paying back the missed payments plus penalties and foreclosure filing costs. In addition, in most states, a borrower can stop a foreclosure process by simply filing for bankruptcy.

Regardless of the hows and whys of exactly what caused you, or your friend, to start missing payments, the best thing to do is to seek the advice of an experienced real estate attorney immediately. An attorney can tell you exactly what the foreclosure process will entail, given the laws of your state, the contract you signed, and the bank's internal procedures. One piece of advice that she may provide is that if you have no way of reinstating your loan, you should sell your home fast. Why? Because once a foreclosure begins, every missed payment, penalty, and foreclosure-related cost is added to the principal balance, meaning that as time goes on, you owe more and more and more to the bank. The longer you wait, the worse it gets. This is exactly why many sellers who need to sell quickly consider using a fire sale to attract an investor.

Fire Sales—Selling Your Home Quickly

In the teeter-totter struggle of price vs. time, a fire sale is just what it sounds like; it's when a seller agrees to reduce his price dramatically in order to secure an offer quickly. Interestingly, it's not just sellers who are in trouble that use fire sales to dispose of real estate. Family members who have had a recent death in the family, corporations that want to remove unwanted real estate holdings from their books, investors who need to complete tax-structured sales, and even just regular sellers who don't want to spend several weeks or months marketing their home often use fire sales to complete their real estate transactions quickly. Just like paying to be placed in the front of the line at your favorite sporting event, sacrificing a portion of your purchase price can move you to the front of the real estate market.

The critical question for any seller considering a fire sale strategy is, how deeply do you cut the price? Obviously you don't want to give

STRATEGY 44

To sell quickly, try
using a fire sale
approach to
attract investors.

up more than you have to, but on the other side
of the fence, if you don't cut deeply enough, you
may not generate enough interest and excitement to sell the home. To help determine your
fire sale price, consider these four important
points:

1. *Loan and lien repayment.* Your first priority is to pay off all the existing loans and liens against the title. Your mortgage, for example,
is a loan against the property that must be repaid at closing. Some
homeowners may also have a second, or even a third, mortgage to
consider as well. In addition, you may have liens against the property; a lien, like a loan, is typically an assessment or court judgment that is filed against the title of the property. These may
include tax liens, utility liens, or even child support payments. All
loans and liens must be paid at closing to deliver a free and clear
deed to the new owner. To check what loans and liens there may
be against your home's title, talk to a local title company about
getting a preliminary title report.

2. *Penalties.* If you have fallen behind on your mortgage payments or
other debts that are secured by the property, it's important to include the total amount of penalties in the payoff. These penalties
will almost always have to be paid at the time of closing to clear
the title. To discover your total payoff, including principal, interest,
and penalties, ask your bank for an estimated payoff statement.

3. *Closing costs.* When you sell your home, the paperwork will typically
be handled by an escrow or title company. This company charges a
fee for providing these services. In addition, a seller will often be
asked to provide title insurance to the new buyer. Title insurance
gives the buyer the assurance that she has received a title that is free
of any defects that could pose a problem later on when she decides
to sell the property. To help budget for this expense, request an estimated closing cost breakdown from your local escrow company.

4. *Professional fees.* Many homeowners will hire real estate professionals to aid them in the sale of their home; these service providers
could range from inspectors to real estate brokers and even a real
estate attorney to help ensure a successful sale. The costs of these
services should be included in the closing costs of the sale.

To put these numbers into perspective, let's look at a real-world closing document (Figure 8-1).

Figure 8-1

	Seller Settlement Statement
	Folder Number: 22-497

Settlement Date: 04/20/06	Disbursement Date: 04/20/06			Final

Name and Address of Buyer(s):

Name, Address of Seller(s):   Investment Property Exchange Services, Inc.
P.O. Box 2653
Salem, OR 97308

Property Location(s):   94 SE Douglas Avenue
Roseburg, OR 97470

Settlement Agent: Ticor Title
1600 NW Garden Valley Blvd., Suite 110
Roseburg, OR 97470-0011

Description	(POC)	Seller Debit	Seller Credit
Contract Sales Price			107,900.00
PRORATION(S)/OFFSET(S)			
County Tax Proration			206.40
04/20/06 to 07/01/06 (72 days) @ 2.866712/day			
RUSA			5.67
04/20/06 to 04/30/06 (10 days) @ 0.566667/day			
BROKER'S COMMISSION			
Total Commission		6,474.00	
Division of Commission			
to All State Real Estate			
3% of Sales Price $3,237.00			
Division of Commission			
to Coldwell Banker NWP			
3% of Sales Price $3,237.00			
PAYOFF(S)			
Oregon Department of Transportation		64,058.74	
Principal $63,687.95			
Interest $370.79			
TITLE CHARGES			
Basic Escrow Rate		184.00	
to Ticor Title			
Title Insurance			
Standard Owner's Policy		475.00	
Coverage $107,900.00			
Premium $475.00			
to Ticor Title			
Municipal Lien Searc		25.00	
to Ticor Title			
Overnight Postage Fee		15.00	
to Ticor Title			
GOVERNMENT RECORDING AND TRANSFER CHARGES			
Record Fulfillment Deed		26.00	
to Ticor Title			
ADDITIONAL SETTLEMENT CHARGES			
Pay Account Current		34.00	
to Roseburg Urban Sanitary Authority			
Exchange Fee		250.00	
to Investment Property Exchange Services, Inc.			
Due From Seller		71,541.74	
Total Paid By/For Seller			108,112.07

Due From Seller		71,541.74
Total Paid By/For Seller		108,112.07
Net to Seller		36,570.33

The most important number on this net sheet is the last one—the "net to seller" figure. This is what the seller receives at closing; it's not a lot of dough, but in this transaction, the seller, yours truly, needed to sell quickly to complete a 1031 tax-deferred exchange (a special provision in the tax code that allows investors to roll their capital gains from one investment property into the next as long as they adhere to some special rules). To accomplish this goal, I reduced my asking price to a fire sale price and let the offers fly.

One big danger for sellers in setting a fire sale price is assuming that the equity in their home or investment property will solve every financial problem that they have. Their reasoning often goes something like this: Well, if we sell the home, we can pay off the credit cards, both cars, the boat, and the RV, and then we'll be debt free! The trouble is, sellers who think that just because they need a certain amount of money out of their home sale, they will get it are in the same position as a guy who thinks that if he buys enough lottery tickets, he's bound to win. The odds are strongly against it.

It really doesn't matter how much you as a seller need; what really matters is only what you can realistically get. This is especially true when you are considering a fire sale. To be attractive enough to lure investors out from the dark corners of the market, your home will have to be priced below market value. This means that you will be giving up some of your equity in exchange for a faster sale. The faster you need to sell, the more equity you may need to give up (see Figure 8-2).

Figure 8-2

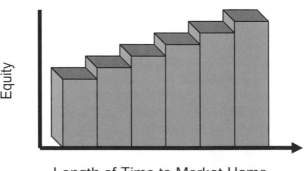

Length of Time to Market Home

The less time you have to market your home, the less equity you can expect to net from the sale.

Once you have set your fire sale price, it's time to tell the world because you now have a unique advantage over your competition. You can now offer buyers something they can almost never find: instant equity.

Advertising to Attract Bargain Hunters

Once you've decided to sell your home in a hurry, it's time to tell the world about it. After all, offering your home at a fire sale price and then not marketing it aggressively is like cooking a huge meal and then not inviting any guests to attend. It's a complete waste of time and energy. You must advertise far and wide the fact that your home is now available at a deeply discounted fire sale price. How? Let's take a look at five ways to get investor bees buzzing!

1. Rewrite Your Advertising Copy

The first step in attracting real estate sharks is to let them smell blood in the water. How? By rewriting your advertising copy to target bargain hunters and investors. For example, take a look at how a standard advertisement targeting first-time home buyers is transformed into a fire sale advertisement.

Standard Advertisement:

Ring the Dinner Bell—Afterward relax in the attached family room, or move to your own covered patio. With spacious bedrooms and an extra half bath, this home is perfect for 1st time home buyers. Seller will even help with closing costs!—$395,000 Call 1-888-555-1212 to learn more!

Fire Sale Advertisement:

Motivated Seller—Medical emergency forces the sale of this newer home on the Westside. Seller has deeply discounted the price and is ready to review offers. Home offers family room, covered patio, spacious bedrooms, and an extra half bath. Won't last long call today!—$295,000 Call 1-888-555-1212

Notice that the second advertisement isn't coy; in plain English, it announces to the world, "I need to sell this home fast!" In a fire sale

STRATEGY 45

When advertising to attract investors, be direct; let them know that you are motivated to sell quickly.

situation, you have to be direct. All question marks must be removed. Nothing can be left to the imagination. Investors and bargain hunters need to know exactly why you are selling and that you are ready to review all offers. To leverage this technique, take a look at several headlines that may attract the attention of buyers looking for a bargain.

- Must Sell Now
- Preforeclosure Sale
- Prebankruptcy Liquidation
- Home Liquidation
- Equity Sacrifice
- Instant Equity
- Motivated Sellers
- Bring All Offers
- Desperate to Sell
- Investor Special
- Bargain Hunter's Dream
- Flip This House

Some sellers may wonder, "Do I really want to show all my cards by using such bold headlines?" The answer is yes. A seller who must sell quickly doesn't have the luxury of bluffing. He can't pretend to have a straight flush while actually holding only a pair of twos. No, the best play in a fire sale situation is to lay your cards on the table, tell everyone the truth, and let the highest bidder take the chips. This doesn't mean that you throw away all the equity in your home, but it does mean that you explain clearly your willingness to discount the price to a reasonable level in order to secure a faster sale.

The advantage of this approach is twofold. First, it will attract a much higher number of buyers to your home—everyone loves a bargain, especially a bargain on such a high-ticket item as a house. But second and more important, when investors and bargain hunters find a home that is priced below market value, they often compete to purchase the home. This bidding war can be extremely valuable to a seller who needs to sell fast.

2. Encourage a Bidding War

A bidding war starts when two buyers want to purchase the same home. In some markets, bidding wars have involved hundreds of buyers, all competing for just one home. If you anticipate that your home in your market has the potential to create a bidding war, you may want to follow the advice of Doris, a top-producing real estate agent from southern California: "When I have a home that I know is going to generate multiple offers, I explain to all the buyers and their agents that we will be reviewing and responding to all the offers on a certain date, normally about a week after I list the property. Because of this, they should make their highest and best offer."

She then includes a statement in the MLS system that says:

MLS DATA SHEET—SAMPLE

Remarks: The sellers will review and respond to all offers on X date. Please make your highest and best offers to ensure acceptance.*

*This is used as an example only. Consult with a local real estate professional or attorney when developing an MLS strategy that encourages multiple offers.

In addition, savvy sellers instruct their agents to make an announcement at office and MLS meetings to inform the real estate community of the seller's need to sell quickly and his willingness to discount the price. For instance, an agent might say something like: "I've just listed a home at 123 Johnson St. The seller has given me written permission to let you know that this is a divorce sale and that both parties are extremely motivated to sell this home quickly. The seller has set a price 10 percent below the market price and is willing to review all offers. If you have any investors or buyers looking for a bargain, this could be a great opportunity."

Surprisingly, however, in many cases a listing agent may be unable to promote your fire sale. Why? Because in general, real estate agents have a fiduciary duty not to disclose a seller's motivation or willingness to accept anything less than full price for her home. By doing so, they would be violating their legal obligations. To overcome this hurdle, you may need to untie your agent's hands by providing him with a written letter of authorization. For instance, the authorization letter may be as simple as:

ATT: Superstar Sally
ABC Realty
123 Johnson St.
Firesburg, OR 97470

Dear Sally,

Please accept this letter as our authorization to begin advertising our home for sale at the newly discounted price of $295,000. As you know, we need to sell this home quickly.
  You may also advertise and disclose to all buyers, agents, and brokers our willingness to review any and all offers and our reasons for selling. Please use any means of marketing necessary to attract buyers to our home, including headlines and ad copy that disclose our need to sell quickly.

Thank you for your help.

Jim and Mary Sellers*

*Consult with your real estate agent or broker about exactly what needs to be included in a "fire sale" authorization letter in your state.

Occasionally a seller will ask me, "Why don't we just leave the price the same, but you can tell buyers to make me an offer? I won't refuse any reasonable offer." This sounds like a grand idea; the problem is that in an MLS system with hundreds or even thousands of agents, it's almost impossible to tell everyone. No, the only way to grab these agents' attention is to slash the price so dramatically that they can't ignore it and then market the heck out of the new price. One way to do this is to use investor search tools.

3. Use Investor Search Tools

One way to target investors who are looking for a bargain is to consider listing your home on investor-centric websites like www.foreclosure.com or the larger RealtyTrac (www.realtytrac.com) system. RealtyTrac is the largest database of preforeclosure and foreclosure properties in the nation. With both systems, members pay a fee to search properties that may be soon entering the foreclosure process or are already in the midst of a foreclosure sale. But these sites aren't just a place for distressed properties; members can also search MLS-listed homes and even For Sale by Owner properties. Because of this, sellers who are selling by owner may wish to consider adding their listings to these databases in order to put themselves in front of this active group of real estate investors.

4. Use Signs

Bargain hunters are hard shoppers; they are always in the field looking for the next deal. Because of this, one inexpensive way to market a fire sale price is to add a sign rider to your existing sign. Many successful homeowners have utilized riders that use attention-grabbing phrases like

- Below Appraisal
- Major Price Reduction
- Motivated Seller
- Must Sell Now
- Price Reduced

By using a real estate "For Sale" sign to market your motivation level, you will be able to instantly raise the neighborhood's awareness of your desire to sell quickly. While this can be a little bit embarrassing, it is far better than the alternative of losing the equity in your home. The good news is that bad news travels fast. Is that such a terrible thing? Not really; in fact, according to the National Association of Realtors, in 2006, 8 percent of buyers found their home through the recommendation of a friend, neighbor, or relative. This same approach applies to flyers and Internet marketing.

5. Use Flyers and Internet Marketing

Every marketing piece, whether online or in print, needs to be re-branded with the clear message: I need to sell now! For instance, take a look at how the flyer in Figure 8-3 is transformed from a typical marketing piece into a lightning rod for generating investor interest.

Figure 8-3

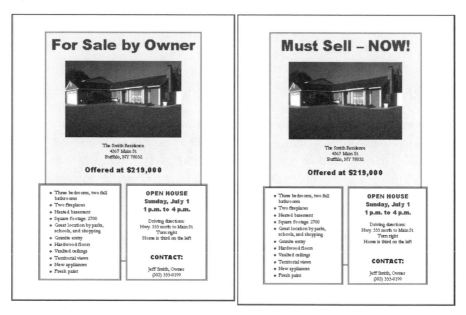

But what if all of your marketing efforts just aren't doing the trick? Your next alternative may be to consider using a real estate auction to sell your home.

Auctions—Selling to the Highest Bidder

According to the National Auctioneer Association (NAA), in 2006, the biggest increase in the entire auctioneering profession was in residential real estate, which grew by 12.5 percent and generated $16 billion in revenue. Bill Sheridan, 2007 president of NAA and a licensed real estate agent since 1975, explains, "When you list a house, you don't know when it's going to sell or for how much. If you're in a seller's market, the house may go quickly. But if you're in a market like we are in now in much of the country, sellers don't know how long it's going to take to sell and what the final price will be." The appeal of a real estate auction, he goes on to explain, is that sellers can often sell fast.

> **LUXURY PROPERTY AUCTIONS**
>
> According to the March 2007 *Real Estate Intelligence Report*, real estate auctions aren't always for property owners in distress.
>
> In early 2007, the national auction company J.P. King sold two penthouse condos on Palm Beach's Singer Island. The properties in the Oasis Condominium building went for $2.5 million and $2.4 million. Ten registered bidders participated in the sale, with each bidder being required to present a $50,000 cashiers check to participate.
>
> "We had some pretty envious developers watching," said Craig King, president of J.P. King.

Real estate auctions aren't for everyone. Typically they are best suited to sellers who are willing to accept less than market value for their home in order to sell it quickly. But for sellers who do need to sell fast, they have some distinct advantages. For instance, here are five reasons why many sellers love auctions:

1. *An auction is an event.* It's something that can be marketed easily.
2. *Urgency for buyers.* The auction date creates a deadline for buyers to take action.
3. *Seller control.* By setting a reserve price, a seller can remain in complete control.
4. *Few or no contingencies.* Most auction sales contain few or no conditions of sale.
5. *Fast closing.* Auction sales are typically closed within 30 to 45 days.

A real estate auction, not unlike any other type of auction, starts with a seller, someone who needs to be rid of some unwanted item—in our case, real estate. Next, the real estate is evaluated to determine its market value; typically this is done by using either a standard appraisal or a competitive market analysis. Once the market value has been determined, the seller decides what is the minimum he will accept for the property. This is often referred to in the auction world as the reserve, or the price the seller must receive in order to proceed with the sale. Next, the seller and the auctioneer agree on the kind of auction that best fits the seller's needs. For a guide to the different kinds of auctions that are used to sell real estate, check out the list at www.REALTORauctions.com. It's worth noting that in my own company, our in-house auctioneer, Dean Allison, encourages selling agents to attend with their buyers. This means that if one of these buyers purchases the home, the selling agent who has attended the auction with the buyer will still be paid a real estate fee. Why use this approach? This strategy encourages agents to embrace the auction instead of potentially pooh-poohing it to their buyers.

Depending on the type of auction utilized, once the gavel has sounded and the auction is complete, the highest offer is presented to the seller. If the price has reached the minimum reserve, the property is sold. If it has not, the seller has a decision to make. She can accept the highest bid price or reject it. This is what makes an auction so interesting and so exciting. To find a professional real estate auctioneer in your area, look for one who holds the Accredited Auctioneer, Real Estate (AARE) designation. You can find a complete list at the Auction Marketing Institute, located online at www.auctionmarketing.org.

Now here's a tough question: What if you owe more than your home is worth? While this is never a good position to find yourself in, there may be an answer to this dilemma that just might surprise you.

Short Selling—Partnering with the Lender to Sell Your Home

If you have ever dreamed of trying your hand as a day trader, or even just opened an online stock brokerage account, you may have come across the concept of short selling. Short selling is when an investor sells stock that he doesn't actually own in hopes that the price will fall so that he can then buy the stock back at a lower price and "cover" the sale. Believe it or not, many lenders do something similar with mortgage notes. In lending lingo, a short sale means that a mortgage

STRATEGY 46

Explore a short sale agreement with your lender.

holder accepts less than face value for its note in order to avoid an even larger loss.

For instance, let's say that Bob and Mary, a nice couple from Phoenix, Arizona, purchased a home during the peak of the housing boom for $532,000. To finance the home, the lender recommended an 80/10/10 arrangement. This means that Bob and Mary put 10 percent down on the home, or $53,200, and the lender, Sand Dune Bank and Trust (SDBT), financed 80 percent, or $425,600, on a first mortgage. The remaining 10 percent, $53,200, was financed through a second mortgage from Dune Country Bank (DCB).

Bob and Mary do very well for about a year and make their combined monthly payments with relative ease. But then suddenly Bob loses his job in a massive corporate downsizing. To try to cope with the loss of income, they move out of their dream home and into an apartment. At first they try to sell the house, but they receive only two offers from investors, and they are willing to pay only $510,000 for the property. So they attempt to rent the home, but because their payments are so high, the rent needs to be so steep that no one is willing to pay it.

Soon they receive their first notice of default, and then several more from both SDBT and DCB. These are peppered with demands for immediate payment, and these are followed up by phone calls from empathetic, yet firm, bank officials who outline how Bob and Mary's credit will be ruined if they don't find a way to make up the missed payments quickly. At this point, both banks have several different options to consider:

- *Foreclosure.* The banks could proceed with a foreclosure and attempt to recoup as much money as possible.

- *Forbearance.* Depending on the terms of the note, the lender or servicer may agree to forbearance, meaning that Bob and Mary will be given a few months to find a job without making payments. Often these delinquent payments are then added back to the principal. Unfortunately, neither SDBT nor DCB will agree to forbearance.

- *Restructure.* Sometimes referred to as a workout, this is where the bank offers to rewrite or restructure the note, but with Bob still unemployed, this is highly unlikely.

• *Deed in lieu of foreclosure.* This option would allow Bob and Mary to sign over the deed to the bank, avoiding the foreclosure process. This can provide substantial savings to the bank, as it doesn't have to pay the attorney fees and other costs associated with an often lengthy foreclosure process. But with two separate banks each holding a mortgage, this is also a highly unlikely possibility.

After three missed payments, SDBT, the bank with the first mortgage, hires an appraiser to evaluate the property. Upon inspection, the appraiser learns that the home has been broken into by local teenagers and has been severely damaged. Her appraisal and estimate of repairs are handed off to a loss mitigation specialist at the bank to evaluate the potential downside the bank is facing. The report shows that the market has cooled and that high-end homes are selling very slowly. The numbers now show that SDBT can expect to sell the home at a fire sale price of $510,000, but only after spending an additional $25,000 to repair the damage done during the earlier break-in. In addition, completing the foreclosure process will cost $35,000 in real estate and attorney fees. Tax liens and holding costs add another $15,000 to the total costs. So in the end the numbers break down as follows:

Sale price:	$510,000
Repairs:	25,000
Fees:	35,000
Holding cost and taxes:	15,000
Total:	$435,000
SDBT investment:	$425,600

As you can see, SDBT has a relatively minimal risk in the property. It will probably break even and recoup its losses if it is forced to foreclose.

But we're missing something. What happened to the second mortgage? The holder of the second mortgage, DCB, still has a large investment in the property, $53,200. But it also has a problem. It is the holder of the second mortgage, not the first. This means that DCB is last in line to be paid. If the holder of the first mortgage forecloses,

DCB's lien is wiped out. The only way for it to protect its investment is to attend the foreclosure auction and buy the property from SDBT. To put this in perspective, DCB will have to pay $510,000 to attempt to recoup its $53,200 investment. Not likely. Dune Country Bank is facing a 100 percent loss. But there is a way out, a way for DCB to avoid a total loss. It can accept a partial payment, or a short sale, to help facilitate a successful closing. For example, if the owners, Bob and Mary, can secure another investor offer of $510,000, there could be several advantages to all parties involved. Let's see how the numbers might break down differently:

Sale price:	$510,000
Repairs:	25,000
Fees:	25,000 (reduced by $10,000—no attorney foreclosure fees)
Holding cost and taxes:	5,000 (reduced by $10,000—no lender holding costs)
Seller proceeds:	2,500
Total:	$452,500
SDBT loan payoff:	$425,600
DCB loan payoff:	$26,900 (short sale agreement)

In this scenario, the second lien holder, by agreeing to accept a short sale, has salvaged 51 percent of its investment. The sellers have even walked away with a small amount of money for their willingness to participate in the sale. The sellers may also receive, as a credit, a refund of their impound account funds. These are the funds held by the bank to pay for things like taxes and insurance. So as strange as it may sound, your lender is your financial partner. In fact, it probably has a much bigger financial stake in your home than you do, so it has a vested interest in helping you get the home sold.

Of course, it isn't all roses and sunshine. There can be downsides for borrowers who use a short sale. For instance, under certain circumstances, the debt forgiven by the bank may be taxable to the borrower; a good example might be if you borrowed $25,000 against your house to buy a new boat. Typically you're not taxed on the loan amount because the money will be paid back at some point. But if you end up sell-ing your home, and the bank agrees to forgive a portion of your loan in a short sale agreement, in effect you have just been given free money. The IRS doesn't believe in free money, only taxable income, so don't be surprised if you are forced to pay income taxes on your windfall. (Check with a qualified CPA.)

Also, most lenders won't consider a short sale unless you have a signed offer on your home. This often creates a catch-22 situation that many sellers find frustrating. After all, how can you secure an offer un-less you know how much the lender is willing to discount the note, if at all? To overcome this obstacle, many sellers include a statement in their listing data sheet that says something to the effect of:

> *This home's price is based on the lender's agreement to enter into a short sale agreement. All accepted offers, including full-price offers, will be subject to the lender's agreement to discount the note.* *
>
> *This is used as an example only. Check with a local real estate professional or attorney to create your own conditions of sale.

But what if all roads lead to nowhere—the home isn't worth what you paid for it, the lender won't budge, and the market is stagnating? It may be time to consider taking a loss.

When Does It Make Sense to Take a Loss?

As a new agent in the real estate business, I met a middle-aged cou-ple who needed to sell an older rental home that they had inherited from the husband's recently deceased mother. After asking a few ques-tions, I learned that the home had not one but two mortgages on it that had been used to finance the grandkids' college education.

"Jim, we just want the house sold quickly."

After doing some quick math, it was clear to me that after paying a real estate fee, covering closing costs, and paying off their loans, the sellers were underwater. The home was worth less than their debts and selling expenses. To sell the home, they would have to pay money out of pocket.

"You could go For Sale by Owner, and maybe save the real estate fee," I offered, uncomfortable with seeing anyone have to write a check to sell their home.

"No, we don't have time to deal with buyers. Plus it might not sell, and we need it sold." The wife nodded her head as the husband spoke. It was clear that they just wanted closure. "Listen, Jim, here's the way I look at it. My mom paid for both of my daughters to go to college. So we're not losing any money."

A couple of months later, the sellers walked into closing and wrote a check for over $10,000. In their case, taking a loss was worth more than trying to squeeze money from an asset that simply had no more to give. The property's equity had already been tapped out.

Taking a loss when selling a home is never something that you want to have happen. After all, real estate is supposed to be a safe investment, a wealth preservation tool that should be nearly impossible to lose money on.

While that's often true in the long term, it can be affected by many things in the short term. For instance, a homeowner who bought his home in a peak market cycle may have to wait several years to recoup the costs of his initial investment. If a home buyer purchased a home this year for $225,000, he will probably incur closing costs and financing charges that amount to at least 2 percent of the sales price, or $4,500. If he now decides to sell the property, he will be hit with a new set of closing costs plus the potential for a real estate commission. If these expenses add up to only 6 percent of the sale price, this would equal an additional $13,500. This means that for this seller just to break even, he would need to sell his home for $243,000, or 8 percent more than he paid for it.

This problem can be compounded by a weak real estate market, or even declining home prices. In addition, homeowners who have taken on additional debt that is secured by a second or even a third mortgage can quickly find themselves owing more than their home is worth.

But if a seller can hang on for even just a few years, in most markets the natural and consistent appreciation of real estate will almost always solve all of his woes.

How can we be sure of this? According to the Office of Federal Housing Enterprise Oversight (OFHEO), home price appreciation over the last 10 years has been strong, even after the so-called collapse of the housing bubble (see Figure 8-4). If you take the lowest appreciation

Figure 8-4

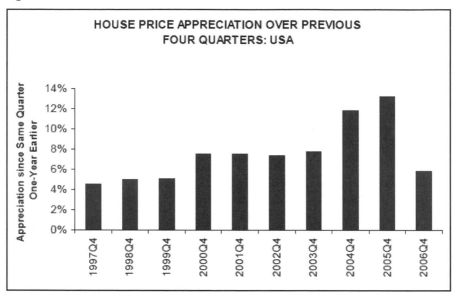

levels of just over 4 percent, our seller in the previous example would be able to break even on his buying and selling expenses in just a couple of years, and this doesn't even count the tax benefits of homeownership or the reduction in the loan principal from making monthly mortgage payments.

Obviously the problem arises when a homeowner is forced to sell his home within a very short time of buying it. In this case, it is often much more difficult to avoid a loss. But believe it or not, taking a loss on a real estate investment can make sense in some cases. Let's look at some of the best reasons justifying taking a real estate loss:

- *Job transfer.* If you have been transferred to a new city, instead of trying to support two households, it can often be less expensive to bite the bullet and sell at a loss. You may find that you can recover the loss in just a few months with your savings. *Advanced tip:* Ask your accountant about the tax deductions available when moving from one city to another because of a job transfer. Also try asking your employer to cover some of your housing-related expenses.

- *Holding costs.* When homeowners add up the cost of mortgage payments, taxes, insurance, utilities, and maintenance, many find that by selling their home quickly, even at a discount, rather than holding out for a higher price that may never come, they may avoid a bigger loss later. *Advanced tip:* Calculate your real estate holding costs by adding up your monthly housing expenses. Next, determine how many months it would take you to recover a loss.

- *Credit preservation.* Homeowners who want to preserve their credit rating by avoiding a delinquency or, worse, a foreclosure may find that it is better to accept a loss than pay for a damaged credit rating for years to come. *Advanced tip:* If you find that you are on the brink of missing a mortgage payment, call your lender and ask for permission to miss a payment or create a payment plan. Almost all lenders will work with you to avoid a delinquency.

- *Peace of mind.* Some sellers find that it is better to wash their hands of the home rather than to continue fighting a losing battle to sell it. Because of this, many families find that writing a check at closing is a far better choice than enduring the emotional toll that an unsold home can wreak on a marriage. *Advanced tip:* Some sellers find it wise to poll the family to determine whether it is worth the effort to attempt to hang tough and wait for a potential buyer or whether they should cut their losses and move on.

Now I'll give you a confession. I've lost money on real estate. Yep, even though I'm a seasoned real estate professional who has bought and sold millions of dollars' worth of homes over the years, I've stepped in a big pile of whoops a couple of times. While I'm never excited about losing money, in each case where I was forced to take a loss, I gained something far more valuable. I gained knowledge.

When considering your own situation, measure the pain of staying on as an owner against the pleasure of being released from the responsibility. Freedom can be priceless. Both times that I lost money on real estate investments, I was happy, even ecstatic, to be free of the responsibility. Not only were the properties a drain financially, but they were also a mental anchor. They were something I thought about constantly day and night. They tied me down and held me back. Being free of both of them was worth every penny of the loss.

To help them evaluate these big decisions, many sellers find great value in leaning on the advice of a competent real estate professional.

In addition to helping you analyze whether you should sell at a discount or hold out for top dollar, a competent professional can often provide you with invaluable counsel during a negotiation, because once you do get an offer, the big question is, what do you do next? How do you evaluate and respond to a buyer's offer? Let's explore this critical issue in Chapter 9, "Evaluating Offers and Managing Transactions."

Evaluating Offers and Managing Transactions

It was once said that the only two things you can be sure of in life are birth and death because everything in between is a negotiation. This is certainly true in the real estate business. For both real estate agents and private sellers, there are many times when negotiating becomes a critical part of the sales process. From simple things like attempting to secure an appointment with a buyer to negotiating an offer or counteroffer, talking to contractors, or even defusing a transaction crisis, your negotiating skills can be a critical component in the successful sale of your home. This may be one reason why, according to the annual *Profile of Home Buyers and Sellers* compiled by the National Association of Realtors in 2006 (www.REALTOR.org), homeowners rated an agent's ability to negotiate effectively as one of the most important reasons for hiring a real estate professional.

Regardless of whether you hire a real estate professional or go it alone, you as a seller can prepare yourself for a negotiation by starting with some basics, beginning with a better understanding of the sales process. To help, let's take a quick look at the sales process from offer to closing:

- *Preoffer consultation.* If you are working with a real estate agent, ask to review a copy of the standard real estate sales agreement forms used in your local market before you receive an offer. Reviewing these often lengthy documents and asking questions in advance will let you feel more at ease when you do eventually receive an offer.

- *Offer review.* All offers are good, even those that don't meet your criteria for acceptance, so don't shoot the messenger when your agent brings you a poor offer. This can be tougher than it sounds, as in some markets buyer's agents will be allowed to present the offer to you directly (with your listing agent present).

- *Offer response.* You have three choices when responding to an offer. You can accept the offer as written, reject the offer, or counter the offer. Often an offer will include a time limit for response, so be prepared to make a decision quickly.

- *Acknowledgment.* Once an offer or counteroffer has been accepted, the other party generally then acknowledges that a successful negotiation has taken place and that all parties have a "meeting of the minds."

- *Disclosure review.* Sellers are generally required to disclose what they know about the home and its material defects to a buyer before closing. This may occur before an offer is written, immediately after the offer is written, or during the escrow period. In most cases, acceptance of a disclosure statement is a condition of the sale, so the statement must be signed by the buyer before a sale can proceed to closing.

- *Condition or contingency removal.* Almost every sale has contingencies or conditions that must be met prior to closing. These can range from the buyer's ability to secure financing to inspections or even lender-required repairs. Because conditions or contingencies must be satisfied prior to closing, sellers are wise to work hard to remove them as quickly as possible.

- *Final walkthrough.* In most areas, a buyer will be allowed to conduct a final walkthrough of the home prior to closing. This prevents the buyer from being stuck with a home that has deteriorated or been damaged during escrow. Because of this, in most areas of the country, a home must be in "substantially" the same condition as when the buyer first viewed the property.

- *Closing.* The closing of the transaction will generally occur in either an attorney's office or an escrow company's office. In both cases, the seller will be signing over her interest in the property in exchange for the purchase price minus closing costs. To avoid surprises, ask your escrow agent to provide you with an estimated closing statement. This will provide you with a rough idea of your net proceeds.

Of course, just because I understand how a dentist pulls a tooth doesn't mean that I necessarily want him handing me the pliers, which is why for many sellers, negotiating a transaction is something that they never want to tackle. Rather, they prefer to be the decision maker, the person who gives each deal the ultimate thumbs-up or thumbs-down signal, while a real estate agent handles the actual negotiation process. But how do you know if a deal deserves the nod? The first step is to establish your decision touchstone in advance.

The Decision Touchstone

When it comes to what we will accept as a price for our home, we tend to be revisionists. For many people, including me, this means that we start with a firm "We won't accept a penny less," move to a more balanced "We'll evaluate each offer as it comes," and finally go to a desperate "We'll look at all offers; just bring us something!" The difference is often our state of mind or what emotional space we occupy when an offer finally arrives at our front door.

While logically you and I know that what is happening in our daily lives should have absolutely nothing to do with what we will accept as an offer for our home, for many sellers this just isn't true. Instead, these sellers allow the mundane minutiae of everyday life to cloud their thinking process; they become infected by the unimportant, and they fall victim to becoming decision makers who are incapable of rational thought. Sound crazy? It isn't. Let me give you an example.

> **The seller is David, a single father, who is raising two teenage daughters and needs to sell because of a job transfer. David doesn't know it yet, but at 4:00 p.m. today, he will receive an offer on his home. Will he accept it, reject it, or counter it? In**

large part this will depend on his state of mind. Let's take a look at his day leading up to the offer.

David wakes up late; his daughters missed their curfew the night before, leading to a huge fight that kept him up until 1:00 a.m. After dropping the girls off at school, he hurries to make it to work on time. Running a yellow light, he draws the attention of a motorcycle patrol officer, who cites him and then with a smile wishes him "a good day."

It's not. He arrives at work late and is reprimanded by his boss. During lunch he grabs his mail and, while eating a quick bowl of soup, learns that one of the letters is from the IRS. He is being audited. The auditor will be calling soon to make an appointment.

Finally some good news: At 4:00 p.m., his real estate agent calls to report that an offer has been made on the house. It's his second offer in two months.

So what do you think? Will David be influenced by his incredibly bad day when he reviews the offer? For most of us mere mortals, the answer would be yes. Not because we want it to, but because it's natural. When we have a bad day, it rubs off on everything we come into contact with. People can see it in your face, in the way you talk, and even in the way you stand. Your mood is more than the way you feel; it's the way you interact with the outside world. Of course, this presents an enormous challenge when reviewing an offer because if we allow our state of mind to influence our decision making, it can potentially cost us thousands of dollars during a negotiation. Worse yet, it can cost us a sale.

Successful sellers don't allow a bad day to negatively influence a negotiation. Instead, they use a decision touchstone as the measuring stick by which to evaluate each offer unemotionally.

In ancient times, a touchstone was a literal stone, such as jasper or basalt, that was often used to test the quality of gold or silver. Likewise today, your decision touchstone can test the quality of a buyer's offer. To build your own decision touchstone, first identify what goals you wish to accomplish as a result of the sale of your home. For instance, let's look at David's goals. He has three:

1. To net $40,000 to $50,000 from the sale of the home.
2. To relocate to his new job by no later than June 30.
3. To have the fewest headaches possible. (A cash sale would be great.)

David knows what he wants, and wisely he has laid these things out in a priority list, starting with netting $40,000 to $50,000 from the sale of his home. Notice that he hasn't named a specific number. This is a wise decision. Sellers who set a price in concrete often face disappointment and frustration by not giving themselves the opportunity to be flexible on other issues. For instance, in David's case, what if a buyer rolled in who offered cash (less headaches) and would agree to close by June 1, but would only agree to pay him enough to net $42,000 from the sale?

> **STRATEGY 47**
>
> Build a decision touchstone in advance of receiving your first offer.

Should he take the offer? Based on his decision touchstone, the answer would be a resounding yes. Of course, many offers aren't as clean as the one David just received. Often buyers will write offers that contain contingencies or conditions of sale that can be a challenge to satisfy, they may make an offer for less than what you had anticipated selling for, or they may make an offer that doesn't fit into your timeline. So even when you revisit your decision touchstone, you may still be left scratching your head. What then? Should you reject the offer? Not yet.

Successful sellers follow the advice of some of the best negotiators in the world by establishing a negotiating position based on an understanding of their own best interests. How can you follow their example? By asking yourself, what if?

The Most Important Question in a Negotiation: "What If?"

Okay, *what if* you're taking your morning swim through the swamp behind your Florida vacation home and an alligator snaps onto your arm? What do you do next?

Authors Joshua Piven and David Borgenicht have the answer. In their book *The Worst-Case Scenario Survival Handbook,* they explain: "If its jaws are closed on something you want to remove (for example, a limb), tap or punch it on the snout." Although the book is presented as a humorous guide, the authors did take the time to consult experts on everything from landing a plane to jumping from a motorcycle to a moving car, and even winning a sword fight.

While we probably won't enter into a sword fight with a buyer, the truth is that great negotiators ask themselves the *what if* question as a way to determine their own best interests and establish a negotiating position. For instance, a wise seller might ask himself:

- What if I don't sell my home to this buyer? What is the next best possible outcome?

And the reverse:

- What if I don't sell my home to this buyer? What is the worst possible outcome?

The easiest trap for sellers, myself included, to fall into is to assume that we are in a strong negotiating position when in reality we are in a very weak position. One of my most memorable examples of this was during my first year in the real estate business.

The home had been on the market for four and a half years before I had the pleasure of listing the property. Small but solid, the ranchette included 40 acres of timberland, a year-round creek, and a good well. Still, no one had been able to sell it. The five sellers, all over the age of 65, had all grown up on the family farm, so, as you might guess, their emotional attachment to the home was strong. Still, everyone was committed to selling, and we quickly set an asking price of $79,900 (don't be too shocked; this was 1989).

After a month of my best efforts, I showed the home to a buyer who, to my surprise, immediately wrote an offer. Bursting with excitement, I called each of the sellers and set an appointment that night to present the offer. Three hours later, I could hardly contain my excitement as the family fanned out around the kitchen table.

"The buyers offered $70,000," I began. "This is a cash sale, so they don't require any financing and they can close quickly." Before I could continue, the objections began.

"That's way too low."

"The home has a new roof."

"The well produces 40 gallons per minute!"

I was momentarily stunned. The sale was going to fail before it even got started.

"Wait," I stalled. "I don't want you to make a decision tonight. We have a couple of days to respond. Let me talk to my broker, and we'll meet again tomorrow afternoon." Reluctantly, the family agreed to sleep on it, and the meeting quickly adjourned.

Rushing back to the office, I met with my broker, who gave me some sage advice. He said, "Jim, you need to show them why they should sell. All they can see now is why they shouldn't." He then went on to demonstrate with pencil and paper a very simple yet powerful way of evaluating exactly what was at stake.

The next afternoon, I was ready to help the sellers evaluate the offer rationally by pointing out both the best-case scenario and the worst-case scenario for selling their home. I did this by providing each member of the assembled group with a breakdown of exactly what owning the home was costing them (see sidebar). The breakdown started with the price the buyer was offering, then gave an analysis of what owning the home was costing the family

COST OF OWNERSHIP	
$70,000	Offer
$3,500	Interest lost (5%)
1,200	Taxes
500	Insurance
500	Maintenance
500	Utilities
$6,200	Total annual cost

each year. The first line, I explained, contained the interest lost, or the amount of interest the family could earn by investing their $70,000 worth of equity into a reasonably safe investment. Next I listed the taxes, insurance, maintenance, and utility costs, and finally I added up the total.

"Today, the home is costing you roughly $6,200 per year to own, or a little over $500 per month. In the four and a half years you have been waiting for this offer, it has cost you $27,900 to own this property."

The members of the group, who had been whispering, suddenly went silent. I had their attention.

"I'll respect any decision you make. But my concern is that if we reject this offer, it might take another four and a half years to generate the next offer. Are you comfortable with that?"

No, they weren't. They took the offer. Why? Because they clearly realized the downside of taking a strong negotiating position when they had no basis for doing so. They understood the *what if* question.

Of course, the reverse of this can be true as well. A great example of this is what happened to one of my good friends and agents, Bob. Bob came to me one morning after an offer he had written had been shot down. He was angry. "I can't believe that the seller's agent didn't even bother to make a counteroffer. I think it's unprofessional."

Bob had written an offer on a home in an exclusive area of town called Laurelwood, a neighborhood of highly sought-after vintage homes. His buyers, like many others, were committed to buying in Laurelwood, so when this home had come on the market, they had immediately sprung into action by viewing the home and quickly writing an offer. But instead of writing a full-price offer, they offered slightly less than full price.

"Will the buyers consider any other areas of town?" I asked, already guessing the answer.

"No, they want Laurelwood."

"Have you tried searching For Sale by Owners or expired listings in the neighborhood?" I offered.

Yes and yes, and no there weren't any homes available. The only alternative was becoming obvious. Bob's clients would have to either pay full price or lose the home. In this case, the sellers were in a terrific negotiating position. Because of the high demand for homes in the neighborhood and the relatively low supply, they were able to command full price for their home.

STRATEGY 48

When evaluating others look at best-case and worst-case scenarios.

Based on your own answers to the *what if* questions, ask yourself: *Am I in a strong negotiating position or a weak negotiating position?* Of course, before accepting any offer, wise sellers take into consideration the overall market conditions, as well as the five essential "must haves."

The Five Essential "Must Haves" You Need Before Accepting Any Offer

There are things in life that just naturally go together: chocolate cake and an ice-cold glass of milk, apple pie and vanilla ice cream, a maple bar and a steaming hot cup of coffee. Likewise, in real estate, there are some key essentials that should accompany every offer. These five essentials help to ensure a smoother, easier transaction, a sale without any of the nasty speed bumps that can slow down or even derail a sale. Can you sell a house without them? Sure, and you can also drive across the country and never put on your seat belt, but why would you?

Let's take a look at the five essential "must haves."

1. A Substantial Earnest Money Deposit

In most areas of the country, when a buyer presents an offer on a home, it is accompanied by an earnest money deposit. Earnest money is just what it sounds like: a deposit that shows a buyer's sincerity in closing a sale. If the seller accepts the buyer's offer and she then backs out without cause, the seller may be able to collect this deposit in exchange for having held the property off the market. On the other hand, if the buyer withdraws from the sale because of a legitimate condition of sale that is included in the offer, for instance, securing financing, she may be able to get a full refund of her earnest money. During the escrow period, the deposit is generally held by a neutral third party like an escrow company and then applied to the purchase price at closing.

For you as a seller, the larger the deposit a buyer makes, the more serious and committed that buyer is and the better you should feel. On the other hand, a small deposit, or, worse, a promissory note, may indicate a buyer's unwillingness to fully commit and put anything at risk. Decide in advance what you feel is an appropriate earnest money deposit relative to the price of your home.

2. A Preapproved Loan

Several years ago, I sold a home for one of my secretaries, Mary. She and her husband were relocating to a new city on the Oregon coast. They weren't in a rush, but they did want to sell relatively quickly.

The home, a single-level ranch-style home with three bedrooms and one bath, was in a nice neighborhood close to schools, shopping, and services, so it was no surprise that within a week of listing the home for sale, we received several offers. After carefully screening the offers, we selected what we thought to be the best of the bunch. Unfortunately, 30 days later, on the day of closing, I got a call from the buyer's agent explaining that the loan hadn't passed underwriting. The sale had failed.

Furious, I wanted to blame everyone—the buyers, the lender, even the other agent. But in truth, I had failed the sellers. How? By not requiring that the buyer provide the seller with a letter of preapproval at the time of the offer acceptance. A letter of preapproval states that the buyer has been qualified to purchase the home based on the information that he has provided the lender at the time of the loan application. This doesn't mean that the buyer is fully approved, as the lender still has to verify assets and liabilities, run a credit report, and verify income, employment, and residency, but it does provide a sense that the buyer is a legitimate prospect.

REQUESTING FULL LOAN APPROVAL

Many sellers and their agents go one step further by requiring that a buyer be fully approved for a loan before accepting an offer. Full approval means that the lender has no conditions on financing the buyers other than approval of the home itself. The downside to this approach is that a buyer may want to "tie up" a home before committing himself to a lender. Because of this, a seller who uses this technique may run the risk of losing potential buyers.

---

3. Time Limits for Condition and Contingency Removal

Imagine that you have received an offer that meets all of your needs but that includes a condition that the home be inspected by a licensed pest and dry rot inspector. That sounds reasonable enough, right? Absolutely; almost every buyer will want this kind of inspection. Unfortunately, without a deadline, this condition of sale can come back to bite you. How? A condition or contingency that has not been satisfied means that the buyer still has an opportunity to back out of the sale, potentially without penalty, all the way until the day of closing.

As my old friend Sam, a retired real estate broker, used to love to tell me, "Don't be surprised if you give a rabbit a hole if he doesn't jump down it." Buying a home is a stressful event, so a buyer who has an open-ended condition, one that she can use as an excuse to exit the sale without penalty, may have a sudden panic attack and decide that she should bail out of the sale. To prevent this, wise sellers require that conditions and contingencies be removed as quickly as possible.

> **MOST COMMON CONTINGENCIES:**
>
> Disclosure review
> Financing and appraisal
> Pest and dry rot inspection
> Whole house inspection
> Title approval

4. Clearly Understood Terms of Sale

As a real estate broker, I've reviewed thousands of real estate contracts written both by my own agents and by agents from cooperating companies. The first question I ask myself when studying these documents is this: *Could someone who is not in the real estate business understand this agreement?* If the answer is no, then we have a problem, because people who are not in the real estate business will be reviewing the offer—namely, the buyer and the seller.

A poorly written sale agreement allows room for interpretation. For example, suppose I include a statement in an offer that says "Sale subject to buyer's satisfaction with the heating system." What does that mean? To the buyer, it might mean that he wants a heating system that will heat every room in the house in less than 30 seconds, while to a seller, it might mean that the buyer just wants to ensure that the current system is functional. This condition is open to interpretation. A better version of this contingency might instead read: "Sale subject to an inspection of the heating system showing that the system is fully functional and adequate to heat each room of the home."*

Successful sellers reduce the risk of an offer failing by working with a highly qualified real estate agent or real estate attorney to create agreements that can be clearly understood by all parties in the transaction.

---

* *This is used as an example only. Consult a real estate professional or a real estate attorney to draft real estate sale conditions or contingencies.*

5. Progress Benchmarks

When you paint a house, you can clearly see your progress. As each room changes color, you know that you are one step closer to your goal; each room, then, is a benchmark. But in a real estate transaction, how do you know that the sale is moving forward? If you're using a poorly written real estate contract, you might not know whether the sale is moving forward, backward, or sideways. What you're missing are benchmarks, beacons of hope that signal that your transaction is flying in the right direction and that you are on course for a successful landing.

Thankfully, many standard real estate agreements have built-in benchmarks; for instance:

- Buyer must submit a loan application by a specific deadline.
- Buyer must pay appraisal and lender fees by a specific deadline.
- Buyer must approve a preliminary title report by a specific deadline.
- Buyer must approve a disclosure statement by a specific deadline.
- Buyer must approve inspections or reports by a specific deadline.

RISK MANAGEMENT: WARNING—FOR SALE BY OWNER

If you are selling your home For Sale by Owner, be sure to use a sale agreement that has been reviewed by a qualified real estate attorney. Using a handwritten agreement, an agreement taken from the Internet or from a book, or even a sale agreement provided to you by a real estate agent can be dangerous if the agreement is not filled out properly or does not adequately protect your interests.

STRATEGY 49

The strength of an offer should be measured based on many factors, not just price.

In addition to these often standard benchmarks, some sellers require that buyers become more committed as the sale progresses. An example might be that upon removal of all contingencies, the amount of earnest money must be increased or become nonrefundable. Of course, as a seller, you must carefully weigh any demands you make of the buyer against the real possibility that a buyer may balk and find another home to purchase. Often a good litmus test for determining what you will require of a buyer in a sale agreement is to ask yourself: *If I were the buyer, would I agree to this request?* If the answer is no, don't expect your buyer to agree to it.

Successful negotiators are those people who understand and embrace the simple but powerful techniques that can enable anyone to create a successful sale—the fundamentals.

The Power of Fundamentals

Many real estate agents and even a few home sellers like to think of negotiation as an art form, a talent that you either are born with or must learn through years of intensive training. While intensive training certainly can't hurt, the fact is that anyone can become a better negotiator by applying some simple fundamentals. Let's look at four fundamentals that can give you the confidence to forge the best deal possible:

- *Control your emotions.* Homeowners who become emotional during a negotiation are immature negotiators. Staying in control of a negotiation requires remaining in control of your emotions. Decide in advance that regardless of what is said or done during the negotiation, you will stay focused and positive.

- *Pay attention to the people.* In the end, most negotiations fail or succeed based on how well you can manage people. Ask yourself: Am I paying enough attention to the people in this transaction? Great negotiators are great at reading people.

- *Embrace knowledge.* The person with the most knowledge in a transaction may also be the person with the edge. Make it a goal to become the most knowledgeable person in the room during any negotiation. To accomplish this, be prepared to back up any statements that you make with written documentation; likewise, be ready to refute any claims that a buyer may make with solid evidence.

- *Listen more and talk less.* The best negotiators are the ones who can ask powerful questions, listen, and use silence as a secret weapon.

For anyone who is attempting to buy or sell a home, the scramble to find a negotiating advantage can be an intense, emotionally challenging experience. You, the seller, want to net as much as possible from the sale; the buyers, of course, want the best deal possible; and both of you want the sale closed as quickly as possible. It's no wonder that in many transactions, sellers are forced to make a counteroffer.

The Third Choice: A Counteroffer

You have three choices when it comes to responding to a buyer's offer. You can accept the offer as written, you can tell the buyer to go fly a kite (otherwise known as rejecting the offer), or you can take the third choice and counter the buyer's offer.

While many sellers view making a counteroffer as a natural part of the sales process, what many of them don't realize is that what they are really doing is rejecting the buyer's offer first and then making a new offer to the buyer.

And that's important how?

It's important because if you had accepted the buyer's offer as written, the home would be sold. The buyers would mentally move in and instantly become emotionally vested in the property. Every day thereafter, their resolve would harden, their commitment would deepen, and the odds of the sale closing would widen. When you make a counteroffer, you short-circuit this process. Like a schoolyard bully, you pop the buyers' fun bubble. Now the buyers have the opportunity to run away from the counteroffer or to stand up and trade swings with you. Either way, it's not much fun.

I know that in reviewing an offer, many sellers will find an item that disagrees with them. For instance, a seller might say to herself: *There is no way we can be out of the house within five days of closing; we need at least ten.* The natural next step might seem to be to make a counteroffer asking for the extra time. But the question that successful sellers have learned to ask themselves first is: *Is it really worth a counteroffer?* In other words, is it worth losing a sale over? Perhaps an extra five days to move is worth a counteroffer, or perhaps not—the key is to understand the risk versus the reward.

> **STRATEGY 50**
>
> When responding to offers, ask yourself: Is it really worth a counteroffer?

If you are forced to make a counteroffer, keep these three tips in mind:

1. *Attempt to understand the buyer's position.* A negotiation is never a one-way street. In order to create a sale, both parties must feel that they are receiving a good value. Learn as much as possible about the buyer, his background, and his reasons for making his initial offer. By doing so, you may able to find common ground that can create a successful sale.

2. *Use the give and take technique.* When making a counteroffer, think in terms of not only what you want but what you might be willing to give up to make the sale happen. For instance, if you are asking for a higher price, can you help pay the buyer's closing costs or perhaps pay points to help him secure lower payments?

3. *Emphasize the positives.* In writing your counteroffer, you may want to emphasize the areas that you do agree on before you begin asking for modifications. For instance, point out all the areas of the original offer that are acceptable. These might include the closing date, the possession date, the down payment, the price, the inclusions and exclusions, the type of financing, specific conditions or contingencies, or even something as simple as the size of the earnest money deposit.

Once you do come to an agreement with a buyer, either by accepting her offer or by making an acceptable counteroffer, the home is sold, right? Not yet. You still have to work your way through the escrow process. In other words, you have to manage the transaction.

Seven Ways to Ensure a Smooth Sale

As Emerson once said, "The surest poison—is time." This statement certainly applies to the real estate business because, as most real estate veterans will tell you, the longer the escrow period, the greater the danger of a transaction disaster. To ensure a smoother, faster closing, follow these seven tips:

1. *Collect all of your current loan information.* In order to pay off the outstanding loan and liens that are now encumbering the property, the

closing agent will need to order payoff statements. While it might be natural to think that this can be done with a simple phone call, often a payoff request must be submitted in writing, and it may take a few days to receive an answer back. By requesting a payoff statement early, savvy sellers can avoid a costly escrow delay. The same applies to second or third mortgages, as well as any lien or judgment that is secured against the property title.

2. *Make sure you have the legal authority to sell the property.* If you have inherited the property or been awarded the property in a divorce, or if your spouse has recently passed away, the closing agent will need to collect documentation to prove that you have the legal authority to sell the property. Be sure to ask specifically what documents the agent will need at or before closing. Also, if you plan to use a power of attorney for a family member who is in the title but cannot be present at closing, be sure to ask the closing agent whether the power of attorney will be accepted. In most cases, a power of attorney must be recorded in the county and state in which the sale will be taking place and must provide specific or general powers to sell the property.

3. *Document everything.* If for some reason there is a friendly or not-so-friendly disagreement between you and the buyer about the transaction, how will you resolve it? In a real estate brokerage, we often ask agents, "Can the file speak for itself?" In other words, could a third party reviewing the transaction file determine the intent of the parties without an explanation from either side? If the answer is no, it can spell trouble. To manage these risks, take a look at what should be documented:

- Properly executed sale agreement
- Buyer or seller counteroffers
- Sale addendums or contract changes
- Letters, phone calls, and e-mails
- Reports, inspections, and reinspections
- Escrow files

Sales can be made or lost based on properly documented dates and times. For example, if a buyer has provided a time limit for the seller's acceptance of an offer, the date and time of the seller's signature should be added to the document to prove that acceptance occurred within the allotted time frame.

4. *Track all condition and contingency deadlines.* Many agents and sellers find it wise to create a calendar that tracks all of the contingency deadlines. By using a simple reminder tool, all parties can work together to remove these obstacles quickly and move forward with a successful closing. One easy solution that many sellers and agents use is to enter all of their deadlines into a contact management system.

5. *Quickly complete all necessary repairs and order reinspections.* When an inspector inspects your home, he will find flaws. Your home, like mine and everyone else's, is not perfect. No doubt it has the normal wear and tear, a few oops, and maybe even a few big wows that have accumulated over time. An inspector's job is to look for these problems and report them to the buyer. Depending on the sales agreement, you may be required to fix these items prior to closing. If this is the case, be sure to complete the repairs quickly, if necessary using a licensed contractor, and immediately order a reinspection.

In a reinspection, the original inspector comes back to your home, evaluates the completed repairs, and either tells you to fire your contractor or provides you with a stamp of approval. Once the home has "passed" inspection and the buyers have signed off, you will be one step closer to loading your moving van.

WARNING: LIMITING YOUR LIABILITY

Sellers who agree to complete "all necessary compliance work" can easily find themselves needing medical care when the final bill for repairs is delivered by armored car. To avoid this, wise sellers are careful to avoid giving buyers a blank check for repairs by placing a limit on the amount of money that they are willing to spend.

6. *Stay in the loop.* Some sellers prefer to let the experts handle the details. The trouble is that it's not the real estate agents, or the lenders, or the escrow officers who have the most at risk in a real estate transaction; it's you, the seller (and, of course, the buyers). If the sale fails, all of these other hard-working professionals will move on

to their next sale, but where does that leave you? For many sellers, it leaves them wondering what went wrong and when.

Don't be a bystander in what is perhaps one of the largest financial transactions of your entire life. Get involved, be informed, and stay in the loop. How? The best way is to stay in regular communication with your posse of professionals, including your real estate agent, escrow officer, inspectors, contractors, and anyone else who will have a hand in closing the sale. For instance, take a look at this quick script:

> ### FOLLOW-UP SCRIPT:
>
> *Listen, I want to make sure we have a smooth sale. Do you mind if I give you a call from time to time to check in on the progress of the sale? Thank you!*

7. *Do an early review of the closing documents.* One of the most overlooked steps in a smooth transaction is the early review of all closing documents. By carefully reviewing all of the closing documents, successful sellers may catch errors, see potential problems, and, most importantly, ask any questions that they may have before the day of closing arrives.

Often the most important document for a seller to review is the estimated closing statement or net sheet. This document contains a breakdown of the seller's costs of sale as well as an estimate of the seller's net proceeds from the sale. Don't be afraid to question the numbers. Escrow companies aren't infallible; as a real estate broker, I've personally caught thousands of dollars in net sheet errors in everything from commission rates to tax prorations, and even loan payoff errors.

STRATEGY 51

Careful management of the transaction can help ensure a smooth sale.

Unfortunately, despite your best efforts, it's not uncommon for even the smoothest transaction to hit some turbulence. So what do you do then? Do you pull back, throttle up, and hope for the best, or do you first calmly assess the situation and your options? It's an important decision because the difference in your strategy can avert a transaction disaster.

Five Ways to Deal with a Transaction Crisis

Sometimes closing an escrow is like walking through the forest at night. You have a general sense of where you're headed, but you are also cautious, wary of what might be lurking beyond the trees, ready to spring at you when you least expect it. Of course there's nothing there, but because you're so busy looking for the bogeyman, it's easy to get tripped up by even the smallest change in the terrain. In a real estate transaction, the pressure, emotion, and strain of making a life-changing decision are fertile ground for big problems. To avoid this fate, take a look at how the most skilled real estate agents deal with a transaction crisis.

1. *Step toward the crisis.* When faced with a problem, many homeowners take the ostrich approach to problem solving, meaning that they bury their heads in the sand and hope the crisis will pass. This is the worst possible way to deal with any problem. Any crisis that is left to its own devices will no doubt fester and become much worse with each hour that passes.

As one of my attorneys is fond of saying, "Justice deferred is justice denied." This means that if you wait to deal with a crisis, the home buyer may feel as though she is not being heard, her concerns are not important, and she is not important. Instead, you should face the crisis head on by first listening to the problem and trying to understand exactly what the issues are so that you can then begin to work on the problem.

2. *Define and clarify the crisis.* Occasionally issues get all jumbled up into one big kettle of discontent. To separate fact from fiction and to give everyone involved the best chance at moving toward a successful end result, we need to develop our investigative skills.

How? Simply learn to ask great questions. Many home buyers will feel a great sense of relief when they have been able to vent their feelings and express their concerns. Use this simple list as a guide:

- Encourage: *"Please tell me more . . ."*
- Clarify: *"When did that happen?"*
- Normalize: *"I've had other clients . . ."*

- Empathize: *"I can appreciate that . . ."*
- Solicit: *"I would like your ideas on . . ."*
- Validate: *"I appreciate your willingness to . . ."*

3. *Discuss the issues unemotionally.* This is easy to say and hard to do. As buyers become emotional during a crisis, it's easy to get swept up into the hurricane of emotion. One reason for this is that occasionally people and problems get mixed up together. To separate the two, you may ask the person who is upset this question:

> *"Listen, <name>, it sounds like you're upset; are you upset at me or at the situation?"*

4. *Develop a resolution for the crisis.* I want you to notice that I did not use the word *solution*. A solution often implies that the person with the problem ends up getting exactly what he wanted, and, as we know from experience, this is rarely true. Instead, a professional crisis manager looks for ways to create *resolution*, where both parties may have to give some ground to create an agreement that both parties can live with.

So how do you find a resolution? One way is to simply ask the parties involved. Use this script:

> *How would you like to see this resolved? <Answer> If that's not possible, is there anything else that would make you feel better about the situation?*

5. *Take action now!* Once you have agreement, you must immediately take action. Often we don't necessarily have to create a perfect agreement as long as we are taking steps to move toward a resolution. Most home buyers will recognize that it may take time to resolve a crisis. Often what they want to know is that something is being done to begin the process. To give them a sense of control, you may want to

provide the buyer with updates on exactly what you are doing and what exactly your next step will be. By focusing on the next step, everyone can begin to think proactively and positively.

An hour later we made it to camp, but not before calling ahead to one of our friends who was able to backtrack his way to us using his own lantern. In a crisis, it helps to have friends. The same is true for successful sellers, who often call on the help of a real estate professional to guide them through a transaction crisis.

Now that you have made it out of the woods, it's time to attend the closing. Let's take a look at what to expect on the day of settlement.

The Day of Settlement—Handing Over the Keys

If the sale of your home were a movie of the week, the day of closing would be the final act. Can you see it? The scene would begin with a family hug and then fade into a short package of highlights about your happiest moments in the home. Next would come the tearful close-up, more hugs, and finally the end—a wide shot of the new buyers arriving at the home.

But this isn't a movie, which is why the day of closing is almost always a little anticlimactic. After all, you've already done the hard work—you made the big decision to sell the home, evaluated your competition, set a price, prepared the home for showings, marketed it in every conceivable way, and finally negotiated a fair deal with the new buyers. The exciting stuff has already happened. But the day of settlement is a relief, as if a thousand-pound boulder has been lifted from your shoulders and been transferred neatly onto the back of your new buyers. But wait! We're forgetting something, actually several little things, details that can help the buyers feel good about their shiny new 30-year mortgage.

Why care about the buyers? First, it's the right thing to do, and second, unless you're planning on living on the beach in the Bahamas, you're probably going to be a buyer soon yourself, so it's good form. Let's look at eight ways to make your buyers' life easier:

STRATEGY 52

Make it easy for buyers to make a move.

Eight Ways to Make Your Buyers' Life Easier:

1. *Home keys.* The buyer shouldn't have to hunt down the keys to what is now her own home after closing. Be sure to collect all of the keys and deliver them either to the escrow officer or to your real estate professional.

Special note: Be sure to leave specific instructions that the house keys are to be delivered only after the sale has been recorded and funds have been disbursed. Occasionally overanxious buyers will begin moving into a home, only to discover that they haven't yet taken title.

2. *Garage door openers.* Most sellers leave the garage door openers on the kitchen counter so that the new buyers can easily find and use them. A nice touch might be to install new batteries in the units.

3. *Lightbulbs/air filters.* Imagine buying a new car and finding that the headlights don't work. That would be irritating, wouldn't it? The same is true for buyers buying a home. Why not change any burned-out lightbulbs before leaving the home. If you're really ambitious, change the air filter as well.

4. *Alarm codes.* If you live in a gated community or if your home itself is alarmed, be sure that the escrow officer and/or real estate professionals are given the proper access codes to gain entry into the home. Nothing would be worse for a buyer than being arrested on the first day she moves into her new home.

5. *Cleaning.* The home should be left clean. Many sellers who don't have time to do a thorough cleaning hire a professional cleaning firm to give the home a sprucing up before the buyers arrive.

6. *Utility changeover list.* Buyers relocating from one city to another might not be familiar with the local utility providers. If you leave a copy of your last utility bills or even just a list of local utility companies, buyers will be able to speed up the utility changeover process.

7. *Warranty/system information.* If you have included a home warranty with the sale, leave a copy of the policy number and the service

number with the escrow officer or at the home itself. Also, any appliance warranties should ideally be either attached to or near the appliances or systems themselves.

8. *A gift.* A classy touch for any home seller is to leave the buyers a housewarming gift. This could be as simple as a plant, a bottle of wine, or a dinner for two at a local restaurant. Be creative; the buyers will love it!

Now it's time to celebrate. Congratulations! You've done it—you've sold your home. You've proved that it's possible to sell a home regardless of the market conditions. All it takes is a commitment of time, energy, and hard work.

The Annual Home Tour

At least once a year, my wife and I take a home tour. We don't look at new homes; we look at our old ones, the homes that we have owned over the years. For us, it's fun to look at our life in the context of homes that we have owned.

Each home is like a point on a map, a marker for where you've been and where you're heading, and as much as or more than a home movie or a collection of old photographs, these homes represent something special to me: irreplaceable memories.

Our first stop, and one of my personal favorites, is my old bachelor pad, a condo overlooking downtown, a three-bedroom, two-bath, two-level home with pool access and a deck big enough for even the biggest barbecue. I owned the place for about a year, but I never decorated it or even really ever unpacked. My entire home furnishings consisted of a couch, a bed, a stereo, two chairs, and nothing else. Good times, good times.

A family with a big golden retriever lives there now.

Next, we take a trip past the first house we bought together, the home where my first son was born and learned to walk. I can still see him toddling down the hallways playing hide and seek. I can hear him playing in the bathtub and attacking a pile of spaghetti in his high chair. We laugh about the bright blue exterior that still shows through the paint and the uneven work I did building the cedar fence

surrounding the yard. (It's still standing!) We planted the grass together and walked to the corner store together almost every day.

Our old neighbors are still there; I think they always will be.

A few miles away is the farmhouse we bought shortly after I opened
my second real estate office. It's a tiny house on five acres, nestled next
to a creek and a famous covered bridge. The first day we moved in, an
abandoned cat adopted us. Our son Michael, who was three years old at
the time, immediately graced her with the name Molly, a moniker that
she strangely seemed to recognize. We raised chickens on the property,
and each year wild turkeys would come and stay in the orchard, as well
as deer and a fat beaver. My favorite day of the week on the ranch was
Saturday, my day to cut the grass. I miss my riding mower. I really do.

Today the property is owned by the neighboring rancher.

We end the tour at our current home, a four-bedroom, two-bath
home that we bought from a builder and a client. My second son,
Mathew, born miraculously 10 years after his older brother, Michael,
has never lived anywhere else. Molly still lives with us. The kids play
outside, riding their bikes up and down the streets, and I take care of
the yard. We've replaced the carpet, and I've painted all the rooms, my
office has been remodeled, and the garage is overrun—a typical house.

But you know what? I think it's about time to sell.

Stagnation: What to Do When Nothing Happens!

You started out fired up, excited, and enthusiastic about selling your home. Your family was looking forward to a change in direction, a new beginning, and a fresh start. So you followed everyone's advice to the letter: You priced the home to sell, prepared the home for showings, and even invested in a Web page to help market the home. But now, as you sit by the window watching cars drive by, it's all just very depressing.

What happened?

The first few days after the home was listed were exciting; there was lots of hustle and bustle. First the agent came by, took photographs, and measured all the rooms, followed the next day by her assistant, who installed a lockbox and, later that same afternoon, a brand-new sign. Then there was the Sunday open house, and later that same week an office tour and an MLS tour. But like the wheels coming off a race car, interest in the home skidded to a stop two weeks later. No calls, no showings, no interest.

Congratulations; your home has just been rejected by the market. Ouch! It hurts. I know. I've had many of my own listings rejected by the market during my career. As a seller, your first instinct will be to look for someone to blame, more than likely your real estate agent. That's my first instinct, too; my only problem is that I can't fire myself. I am my own agent! Instead, I have to look around and find out what's going wrong. So before you head to the hardware store for a couple of bags of cement and some fuel for your boat, let's look at some of the reasons why your home may not be being shown, because, believe it or not, it might not be your agent's fault.

Is It Just Bad Timing?

Real estate markets bob up and down like the tide, rising and falling with changes in interest rates, overall consumer confidence, the number of available homes, and even the time of year. This is why many sellers can suddenly find themselves awash in a sea of competition, with no buyers in sight for miles. Because of this, many homeowners try to time the market, and inevitably I'm asked the question, "Isn't it better to sell in the spring or summer rather than the fall or winter?"

Not necessarily. For instance, take a look at the "Inventory in Months" chart provided by the Regional Multiple Listing System (RMLS) of Oregon (Figure A-1), which represents how long the inventory of homes would last if no more new homes were to be listed in the Douglas County market. You might note that in January 2006, the inventory of homes stood at 6.5 months—a number that many agents would trade for in a heartbeat today, but at the time many sellers no doubt thought or said, "Maybe we should wait for spring or summer." Would that have been a good choice? Probably not, because all the way through the summer, market times ticked upward, even during the

Figure A-1

Inventory in Months (Active Listings / Closed Sales)			
	2005	2006	2007
January	3.4	6.5	12
February	4.8	6.2	11.6
March	3.3	6.3	
April	3.1	6.9	
May	3.0	6.0	
June	2.9	8.5	
July	3.0	7.8	
August	3.5	8.5	
September	3.5	8.7	
October	4.6	8.7	
November	4.7	11.1	
December	5.5	11.9	

traditional "busy" months of the year like June, July, and August. Because of this, I often tell sellers who are hesitant to list their home during the winter that they may actually have several advantages over their fair-weather friends. Here are my top 10 reasons for listing in the winter:

10 Reasons to List Your Home During the Winter

1. *Fewer showings.*—Yes, there may be fewer buyers, but the buyers that are left are usually very serious about making a purchase.

2. *Less competition.* Many people wait until spring or summer to list their home, which means that you may have far less competition during the winter than at any other time of the year.

3. *Homes show better during the holidays.* Buyers love homes that can tell a story. The holidays are a great time to show homes because the home is usually dressed up for holiday celebrations.

4. *January is the biggest transfer month.* Did you know that more corporate moves happen during January than at any other time of year? This may be a great reason to list your home during the winter.

5. *Timing.* By putting the home on the market during the winter, you may be able to hit your moving goals more easily.

6. *More time to get top dollar.* By starting to market your home early, you may be able to secure a higher price.

7. *Great time to shop.* If your home sells quickly, you will be able to shop for your next home during the winter; this is a great time to find a bargain.

8. *More advertising.* Because most agents and offices have less inventory during the winter, your home may be advertised more often than during the spring and summer months.

9. *More attention.* Most agents will be able to devote more specialized attention to your needs during the winter because they have fewer clients to manage.

10. *The market.* Today's interest rates are still at 40-year lows. This gives buyers more spending power, which will be even more important when you begin shopping for your next home.

Now I'll tell you a secret: I could make just as convincing a case for listing your home during the spring or summer. The truth is, the best time to list your home is when you're ready to sell. Winter, spring, summer, and fall can all be great times to sell your home. The question here really isn't when you sell; it's how you deal with an overall market slowdown. It's a great question, and one that many agents and sellers are dealing with nationwide.

Overcoming an Overall Market Slowdown

When real estate signs seem to be sprouting from every lawn in your city and the local newspaper is bulging with real estate advertising, it can be easy to think that the market in your area is booming. But in truth, the bigger the local inventory of homes is, the more likely it is that your market is beginning to experience a downturn.

During an overall market slowdown, buyers' enthusiasm for purchasing real estate wanes, fewer homes are sold, and inventory builds up. This excess inventory can cause problems for sellers who are seeking to sell for their home quickly and for top dollar. The biggest challenge is increased competition for the buyers who are still in the market to purchase a home.

Let's look at the top five ways to overcome an overall market slowdown:

1. *Think small.* Savvy sellers have abandoned the idea of attempting to time the overall market and instead focus their energy on their neighborhood or market niche. By identifying and closely monitoring their competition, successful homeowners can stay competitive and proactive. Consider asking your agent to provide you with an update of new listings as they come on the market.

2. *Stand out.* The surest way to stand out in the real estate market is to ensure that your home offers the most overall value to buyers. Value can mean that your home is priced more competitively than your competition, that you are offering more incentives than your competition, or that your home offers superior features and benefits. Ask yourself, if you had to buy another home in your neighborhood, which one would you purchase and why? The answer is the home that offers the most overall value.

> **STRATEGY 53**
>
> Focus on your local competition and offer buyers the most value for the dollars spent.

FIND THE FOCUS FEATURE

Many successful sellers find it helpful to establish a focus feature. A focus feature is one specific feature that highlights your home as unique in the community. Examples might be that your home offers southern exposure, a breathtaking view, or simply an oversized garage. If you differentiate your home from the competition, buyers will have a more compelling reason to view and purchase your home.

3. *Be flexible.* Decide in advance what you can bend on and where you can offer the buyer flexibility. For instance, can you offer immediate occupancy? How about paying points or closing costs? Are you willing to reduce the price for a fast sale? Think ahead, and be ready to make a decision quickly. One tip that John, a top producer from Maine, uses in his MLS data sheets is to include this phrase: "Same day response to offers guaranteed. Seller is available to accept and review offers immediately." Buyers who need to make a move quickly or who want answers fast often appreciate knowing that a seller is ready to respond to offers quickly.

4. *Feed them.* To be memorable, a home must stand out. One way that sellers can help their homes to be remembered is to apply the old adage: *The best way to a salesperson's heart is through his stomach.* After seeing 30 or more homes on an MLS tour, real estate agents may not remember a specific home, but they will remember a good meal. A catered lunch, a homemade dessert, or my personal favorite, an old-fashioned barbecue, will keep agents in your home longer and embed a positive association that they will not easily forget.

5. *One more.* Determined sellers who are committed to selling their home in spite of the market conditions often adopt the *one more* strategy. This means that they will do everything that their competition is doing plus one more. For instance, if your neighbors are doing one open house a month, you do two. If a new listing arrives on the market that is priced more aggressively than your home, you adjust your price. If a seller advertises every week in the Sunday paper, you advertise on Saturday and Sunday. Tony, a real estate agent from Michigan, describes it this way: "I think of it as playing a big game of king of the hill. If you want to sell your home, you have to stay on top of the hill. You have to be the most visible home on the market."

Another way to wash the stink off a stagnating home is to ensure that your marketing ship hasn't sprung a leak, which may be as simple as identifying a simple MLS error. After all, real estate agents today may fill out 5, 10, or even 20 pages of information with a seller at the time a listing is taken. Even if the agent makes no errors, another opportunity for a mistake arises when the information is uploaded into the MLS system by an assistant or MLS data entry person. Additionally, the MLS database itself can become corrupted with bad information or errors. While all of these scenarios are rare, one error can cause a listing to turn from ripe to rotten in a matter of seconds.

Plugging the Holes—Double-Checking the MLS Data

In many ways, the successful sale of your home can be like the sailing of an ocean liner. It's a journey, a voyage from one port to another that can take many days or even weeks to complete. During the trip, you are the captain of your marketing ship; this is true even if you hire a real estate agent to assist you in the sale of your home, because the decisions you make can ultimately determine your success or failure. To begin your voyage, let's look at four details to watch for when it comes to the accuracy of your MLS data.

STRATEGY 54

Be sure your MLS data is accurate and up to date.

1. *Status accuracy.* A listing data sheet with errors can cause a slowdown in showings, or even a halt. One of the biggest culprits can be incorrect status reporting, meaning that a listing is incorrectly listed as contingent, pending, or even withdrawn from the market (see Figure A-2). Agents generally show only active listings. If your home has had a sale failure or if your home was recently relisted, be sure to double-check the status report.

Figure A-2

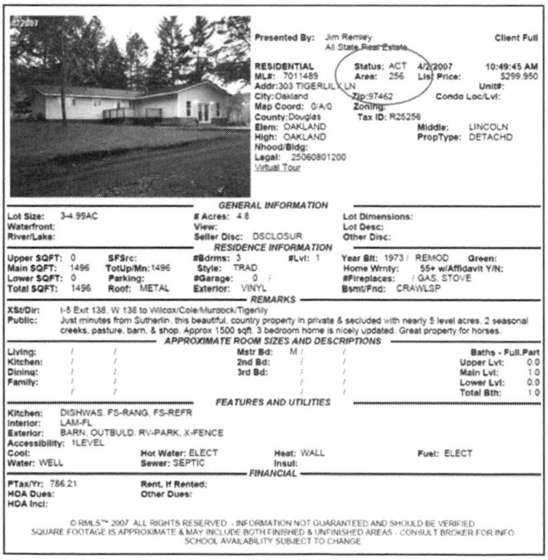
Presented By: Jim Remley, All State Real Estate — Client Full
RESIDENTIAL — Status: ACT — 4/2/2007 — 10:49:45 AM
ML#: 7011489 — Area: 256 — List Price: $299,950
Addr: 303 TIGERLILY LN — Unit#:
City: Oakland — Zip: 97462 — Condo Loc/Lvl:
Map Coord: 0/A/0 — Zoning:
County: Douglas — Tax ID: R25256
Elem: OAKLAND — Middle: LINCOLN
High: OAKLAND — PropType: DETACHD
Nhood/Bldg:
Legal: 25060801200
Virtual Tour

GENERAL INFORMATION
Lot Size: 3-4.99AC — # Acres: 4.8 — Lot Dimensions:
Waterfront: — View: — Lot Desc:
River/Lake: — Seller Disc: DSCLOSUR — Other Disc:

RESIDENCE INFORMATION
Upper SQFT: 0 — SFSrc: — #Bdrms: 3 — #Lvl: 1 — Year Blt: 1973 / REMOD — Green:
Main SQFT: 1496 — TotUp/Mn: 1496 — Style: TRAD — Home Wrnty: — 55+ w/Affidavit Y/N:
Lower SQFT: 0 — Parking: — #Garage: 0 / — #Fireplaces: / GAS, STOVE
Total SQFT: 1496 — Roof: METAL — Exterior: VINYL — Bsmt/Fnd: CRAWLSP

REMARKS
XSt/Dir: I-5 Exit 136, W 136 to Wilcox/Cole/Murdock/Tigerlily
Public: Just minutes from Sutherlin, this beautiful, country property in private & secluded with nearly 5 level acres, 2 seasonal creeks, pasture, barn, & shop. Approx 1500 sqft. 3 bedroom home is nicely updated. Great property for horses.

APPROXIMATE ROOM SIZES AND DESCRIPTIONS
Living: / / — Mstr Bd: M / / — Baths - Full.Part
Kitchen: / / — 2nd Bd: / / — Upper Lvl: 0.0
Dining: / / — 3rd Bd: / / — Main Lvl: 1.0
Family: / / — / / — Lower Lvl: 0.0
/ / — / / — Total Bth: 1.0

FEATURES AND UTILITIES
Kitchen: DISHWAS, FS-RANG, FS-REFR
Interior: LAM-FL
Exterior: BARN, OUTBULD, RV-PARK, X-FENCE
Accessibility: 1LEVEL
Cool: — Hot Water: ELECT — Heat: WALL — Fuel: ELECT
Water: WELL — Sewer: SEPTIC — Insul:

FINANCIAL
PTax/Yr: 786.21 — Rent, If Rented:
HOA Dues: — Other Dues:
HOA Incl:

© RMLS™ 2007 ALL RIGHTS RESERVED - INFORMATION NOT GUARANTEED AND SHOULD BE VERIFIED
SQUARE FOOTAGE IS APPROXIMATE & MAY INCLUDE BOTH FINISHED & UNFINISHED AREAS - CONSULT BROKER FOR INFO
SCHOOL AVAILABILITY SUBJECT TO CHANGE

2. *Incorrect price adjustments.* A price adjust-

ment that is never entered into the MLS system won't help sell your home; likewise, a price adjustment that is entered incorrectly may actually hurt your chances of attracting a buyer. Be sure that your price changes are entered correctly and that they flow accurately across to other advertising media like the newspaper, real estate guides, and other Internet advertising portals.

3. *Accurate showing instructions.* A home that is difficult to show will not be shown. If you have recently made it more difficult to show your home, perhaps because of a change in your working hours, illness, or a visiting family member, don't be surprised if the number of showings goes down dramatically. As soon as the issue has been resolved, be sure to update your showing instructions. Homes most likely to be shown will include these simple instructions: "Call first, then use lockbox." This means that agents will attempt to reach the homeowner first; if she is not at home, they will proceed with the showing by using the lockbox.

SPECIAL NOTE: LOCKBOX PLACEMENT

A lockbox is a small electronic device that real estate agents use to store keys to your home. The box is attached to the outside of your home and is accessible by a master key used only by local real estate professionals. Be sure that your lockbox can be found easily. A lockbox that is hard to find will make it more difficult for agents to show your home. Many sellers place their lockbox on the front door, on the gate, or on a hose bib that is near the main entrance to the home.

4. *Incorrect MLS zone listing.* In most MLS systems, market areas are divided into several smaller MLS zones that become searchable fields. For instance, if I wanted to live at the northwest end of Roseburg, Oregon, I would search in the area indicated on the MLS zone map (Figure A-3) as area 252. But what if a home that is actually in area 252 is incorrectly listed as being located in area 254 (a common

Figure A-3

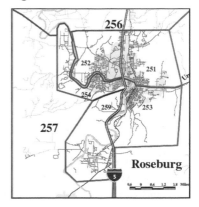

mistake)? The fact is, it would never come up in a buyer's search. Every buyer looking for a home in area 252 would end up missing the listing. Be sure to double-check your home's MLS zone listing.

Now imagine being a deckhand on a cruise liner and discovering that your boat has sprung a leak. Would you pretend you didn't see it and just continue serving the passengers their purple pina coladas? No, I'm sure you would storm into the captain's cabin and tell him the bad news immediately. Unfortunately, in real estate, this isn't always what happens, even when a seller's marketing ship is about ready to take a nosedive to the bottom of the market.

Using the Power of Feedback

As a real estate agent, when you show a home, you can instantly tell if a buyer doesn't like this particular property. It's not so much a feeling as the lack of one, the vacuum of sensing no excitement or enthusiasm about the home. What's harder to pinpoint is exactly what it is about the home that has made the buyers turn up their noses. Was it the green shag carpeting, the wood paneling, the unfinished basement remodeling, or the barking dogs?

To solve this mystery, most selling agents wisely ask their clients to throw them a bone and explain what it is about the house that turned them off. A buyer's answers can often help agents refine their search criteria, saving everyone time and energy. Of course, this doesn't help the poor seller. No, like an overturned turtle, she remains stuck in the same marketing position.

Fortunately, wise agents and sellers can remedy this dilemma by beginning to ask for feedback from both buyers and selling agents. These comments, as hard as they might be to hear, can often be the turning point in helping sellers identify why buyers are rejecting their home. Let's look at two ways to generate a constant stream of valuable feedback.

> **STRATEGY 55**
>
> Use feedback to adjust your competitive position.

1. *Feedback forms.* When a real estate agent shows your home, he is generally required or asked to leave a business card. If you hand over this contact information to your own listing agent, she can then follow

up with either a quick questionnaire over the phone, a fax, or an e-mail to learn the buyer's opinions about the home. Today there are even companies that automate the entire feedback system. For instance, check out the feedback report from www.my feedbacknetwork.com (Figure A-4).

Notice that in this report, all of the buyer's comments are tracked and then placed into a graph format. Seller and agents can even write their own questions to generate even more specific answers.

2. *Real estate agent feedback.* As brutal as buyers can be about your home, no one will be harder on your home than other real estate agents. Real estate agents are a jaded bunch who have seen thousands of homes during their careers, so while they may not say anything unless they're invited to do so, once they've been given permission, grab some tissue and your therapist's phone number because they will have absolutely no problem telling you exactly what needs to be done to sell your home. The question is, how do you get

Figure A-4

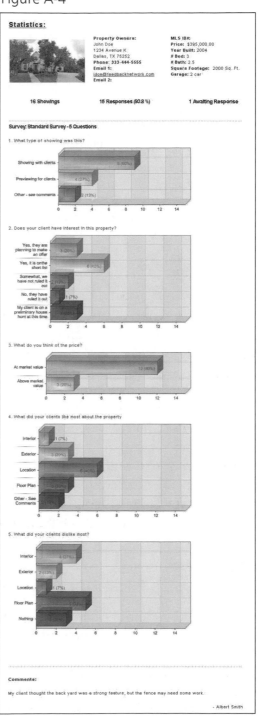

them talking? The best way to discover what local real estate agents think of your home is ask for their opinions during either an office or MLS tour of your home. For instance, you may ask your listing agent to hand each agent an anonymous three-question questionnaire while the agents are visiting your home. Take a look at this sample from Melinda, an agent from Washington State:

YOUR OPINION COUNTS!

Please provide your thoughts about my new listing.

- What do you think this home will eventually sell for?
- Name two home improvements the seller might consider doing.
- Do you think you can sell this home?

Thank you for your thoughts!

Another variation on this same concept is to ask each agent to write a projected sale price on the back of her business card. The business cards are then held, and the agent or agents that come closest to the actual sale price win a prize. The advantage of this approach is that agents who think they can win something may give more time and thought to formulating an answer. The downside is that because the process is not anonymous, some agents may worry about offending the seller.

Assuming that you've now taken all the steps possible to overcome a slowing market, double-checked your MLS data, and, as hard as it was, even listened to the advice of both buyers and agent, but still your home languishes unshown, unsold, and unloved, what can you possibly do next? Believe it or not, quite a bit!

Five Ways to Kick-Start a Dead Marketing Engine

The worst kind of motorcycle you can own is one that won't start. I've owned several, most of them dirt bikes. Hopping on the reluctant beasts, I know that I'm in for a long slog of kicking and screaming, adjusting and readjusting, choking and unchoking, cussing, and then kicking and screaming some more until finally, like a sleeping giant, the bike rumbles to life. As you might guess, occasionally I run into real estate listings that have a similar problem: They refuse to get sold. They should sell; they just don't. Fortunately, I've never owned a motorcycle that I couldn't eventually start, and I've never taken a listing that didn't eventually sell (with or without my help). The key in both cases is to face the challenge head on; after all, walking away won't get the bike started or the home sold.

In facing this challenge, many successful sellers have found that the biggest obstacle in selling a home can often be a dead marketing engine. This means that everything about the home is right on target—the price, the condition, and the selling incentives—but because of a flawed marketing plan, the home is off the radar of the vast majority of buyers. To fix this issue, let's look at five ways to kick-start a dead marketing engine by using the SPARK acronym.

S: Start with the basics

P: Pick a new audience

A: Ask for opinions

R: Rewrite your advertising

K: Kill the stinkers

S: Start With the Basics

More than a few times I have attempted to start a motorcycle, only to find that the bike was completely out of gas. Sellers can fall victim to the same mistake by failing to give their marketing enough fuel, in the form of time and money, to generate interest. A great example is a seller who advertises twice in the local newspaper and once in a local real estate guide, and then declares that his home will "never sell."

Not true! Marketing experts tell us that for any product or service to be "top of mind" in a consumer's consciousness, it may require as many as nine to twelve impressions. An impression is an exposure to your advertisement, which can come in many forms. For example, a seller may market his home in the local paper, in real estate guides, with signs and flyers, with open houses, and even with e-mails to top-producing real estate agents (see Figure A-5).

Figure A-5

STRATEGY 56

Use a burst of advertising in multiple areas to generate interest.

Sarah, a real estate agent specializing in luxury housing, explains it this way: "When I begin marketing a luxury home, I use a burst of advertising, like marketing a movie. I want the property to be everywhere; I want it to be seen by every possible buyer as quickly as possible."

If your marketing has gotten off to a slow start, consider rebooting the plan with a promotion in multiple arenas over a short period of time.

P: Pick a New Audience

What if the burst is a bust? Don't feel too bad; you may have made one of the most common errors in marketing: selecting the wrong target audience. Your target audience is the people you believe will be your most likely buyers.

Agents and sellers either consciously or unconsciously identify a target audience when they write advertising copy, and they inevitably build their marketing plan around the people who they believe will be the most likely buyers for the home. Of course, if they are wrong, they can easily end up spinning their wheels. If your advertising seems to be missing the mark by not attracting buyers, step back and ask yourself these questions:

- Is there another target market that may be more suited to the lifestyle your home offers?
- Have the buyers who have shown interest fit the ideal buyer model you had in mind originally, or did they fit a different demographic?
- Have you tried using multiple target markets by writing ad copy that might appeal to different groups of buyers?

For many sellers, readjusting their advertising focus can be just the ticket for hitting the sweet spot of marketing success.

A: Ask for Opinions

Opinions are like elbows: Everyone's got one, and maybe even two. But opinions, especially when they come from a trusted source, can be helpful when it comes to marketing a home.

Try creating multiple styles of advertising using different headlines, ad copy, photos, and even fonts and colors. Lay them out on your kitchen table and ask your friends and family to give you their assessment. Using this mini–focus group approach can be extremely valuable because, like your friends and family, buyers are real people, not marketing professionals. Your friends and family's reaction to your marketing efforts can provide you with the insight you need to make a change or adjustment in your approach. But be careful: Marketing experts who use focus groups on a daily basis warn of a potential problem called observer dependency that can arise when you are attempting to accurately gauge people's opinions. Werner Heisenberg, the famous German physicist and Nobel laureate, explained this phenomenon as the uncertainty principle. He explained, "What we observe is not nature itself, but nature exposed to our method of questioning." In layman's terms, what marketing experts are warning us of is that we must be careful that when we ask questions, the answers aren't influenced by a person's need to placate us.

A good example might be what happens when my wife asks me how a new dress looks on her. Regardless of what I really think, I always say that the dress "looks fantastic." Our well-meaning friends and family might have the same reaction to a flyer that in reality should be immediately driven to the closest landfill and buried: They'll say it "looks fantastic."

To avoid this false praise, you might ask for their opinion by phrasing your questions in this way:

- You know, there is something wrong with this ad. I just can't quite put my finger on it; can you look at it and tell me what you think?

- I feel like there's something missing from this flyer. Do me a favor; read it over and tell me what I can add.

- Give me some help; what can I do to make this advertisement better?

By framing your question as a cry for help, you can turn a former yes person into someone who gives you valuable advice and insight.

R: Rewrite Your Advertising

How good are you at writing? Some people are natural writers; they enjoy the process of writing, editing, rewriting, and reediting their work until they have created a masterpiece. But for the rest of us who barely passed college English, writing can be a struggle, and ad writing, where you have only a few sentences in which to motivate a buyer to take action, can be seemingly impossible.

The trouble is, a mistake here can mean that the phone never rings. To avoid this fate, some sellers and even some real estate agents employ the services of a professional ad writer or ad-writing system. For example, the company www.writemyads.com allows sellers and agents to enter information about a home, along with photos and feature points, then instantly creates a series of advertisements that can be forwarded to your advertising partners. Check out the sample advertisements for a fictitious home in Tanglewood Heights shown in Figure A-6.

Figure A-6

It's Family Sized	Put Your Name On The Mailbox
Just the right amount of room for the average-sized family in this 3-bedroom/2-bath Colonial home in Tanglewood Heights and only a short walk to the high school. You'll enjoy a casual living room with wood floors, fireplace, built-in bookcases, dining room. $320,000. Please call John Smith for more information.	Of this Colonial brick home in Greenwood. This traditional floor plan delivers 3 bedrooms, 2 bathrooms, master suite with separate shower, linen closet, whirlpool tub, dining room, casual living room with fireplace, built-in bookcases, wood floors, sunny kitchen with breakfast area, walk-in pantry for chips and sodas. $320,000. Please call John Smith for more information.
Formal Dinner Parties	**Feel Safe And Secure**
Are easily accommodated in the formal dining room of this 3-bedroom/2-bath brick home in Tanglewood Heights and only an easy drive to downtown Philly. Great features include a casual living room with wood floors, built-in bookcases, fireplace, master suite with separate shower, linen closet. $320,000. Please call John Smith for more information.	You can rest assured that you'll be alerted with a security system at this Colonial brick home in Tanglewood Heights. This traditional floor plan delivers 3 bedrooms, 2 bathrooms, dining room, master suite with linen closet, separate shower, casual living room with fireplace, built-in bookcases, wood floors. $320,000. Please call John Smith for more information.
Knock On Wood	**Fan the Flames**
You'll feel lucky walking on the wood floors in this 2450-SF home only a short walk to the high school. Features include 3 bedrooms, 2 bathrooms, casual living room with built-in bookcases, fireplace, master suite with separate shower, whirlpool tub, linen closet, dining room. $320,000. Please call John Smith for more information.	For great flavor-filled meals from the built-in barbecue of this Colonial home in Tanglewood Heights and only a short walk to the high school. You'll enjoy 3 bedrooms, 2 bathrooms, casual living room with built-in bookcases, fireplace, wood floors, dining room. $320,000. Please call John Smith for more information.

If you prefer a more old-fashioned approach, open up a local real estate guide and do some R & D—rip-off and duplication. In other words, find advertising copy, headlines, and writing styles that you feel fit your home, and apply a similar approach to writing your ad copy.

K: Kill the Stinkers

One of the easiest things for sellers and real estate agents to do is to become emotionally attached to bad advertising. For instance, a seller who has spent several days writing advertising copy, creating flyers, and building a website may feel so invested in her marketing plan that she resists any suggestion that she change it, even if the

> **STRATEGY 57**
>
> Avoid becoming emotionally attached to any marketing plan.

advertising is producing no results. Successful sellers, though, aren't averse to change.

One way to measure your success is to track every phone call and e-mail that you receive and link it back to the advertisements that you run. Mathew, a superstar in the Portland, Oregon, real estate market, agrees: "Some of my ads will outperform others. The ones that are stinkers I just throw in a file and move on."

Speaking of stinkers, what happens when the advertising isn't the problem, but your home is? This can be a problem, especially if your home has been stigmatized.

Selling a Stigmatized Home

Several years ago near my hometown, a drifter who had been hitchhiking along a major interstate wandered down to a ranch house not far from where he had been dropped off from his last ride. The details of what happened inside are unclear, but what is clear is that while attempting to find a way into the residence, the drifter awoke the owners, there was a struggle, and two shotgun blasts later the homeowners, a husband and wife, lay dead. Eventually the hitchhiker was found and convicted of a double homicide.

Now here is a tough question: Would you buy that home? And an even harder question is: How do you sell it?

This is a classic example of a stigmatized property, or a property whose value has been undermined by a tragic event like a violent assault, rape, murder, or even suicide. For instance, the condo on Bundy Drive in Brentwood, California, where Nicole Brown Simpson and Ron Goldman were stabbed to death, allegedly by her estranged husband O. J. Simpson, instantly became one of the most stigmatized homes in the country. To pay the bills, Nicole's sister Denise was forced to put the condo on the market, where it sat for two and half years before it finally sold for $200,000 less than what Nicole had originally paid for it.

Randall Bell, considered the country's foremost expert on damaged real estate, explains, "Crime scene stigma has two effects on property values. One is the most obvious, and that's the discounting effect. And second is that it takes longer to sell these properties." This assessment is backed up by a study conducted by James Larsen and Joseph Coleman of Wright State University. Published in 2001, the study reviewed 100 "psychologically impacted" houses and found that stigmas reduced the final sales price by an average of 3 percent from market value, but the homes took 45 percent longer to sell.

Many sellers ask, "Can't we choose not to disclose the issue?" Surprisingly, in many areas of the country, the answer is yes. State laws vary, but in many areas a seller may not be required to disclose that a violent crime or a suicide occurred within their home. Similarly, they may be able to instruct their agent not to disclose the stigma to a potential buyer. But be warned: This is threading a dangerous needle. To put this in perspective, imagine that you are an out-of-state buyer who stumbles into a home that seems like a fantastic buy, almost too good to be true. You quickly write an offer, and within 30 days the home is yours. The bad news comes after you move in, when the neighbors inform you that the home was the site of a brutal assault. How would you feel? Upset, angry, or even betrayed? How about litigious?

Regardless of state laws, a seller who chooses not to disclose a stigma to a buyer may later be accused of withholding a material fact. A material fact is considered to be any piece of information that would affect the willingness of a reasonable person to buy a property or would change the amount that person was willing to pay. Of course, these are legal arguments, which is why if your home is stigmatized, you should always consult a qualified real estate attorney.

One area where there is no ambiguity is the issue of people with AIDS or who are HIV positive living in a home. The U.S. Department of Housing and Urban Development has declared that it is illegal to disclose that a current or former occupant of a property has AIDS or is HIV positive. This doesn't make it illegal for a buyer to ask the question, but it does make it illegal for a real estate agent to answer it. It also relieves the seller of any responsibility for disclosing the issue to potential buyers.

Now the big question: How do I sell my home if it does have a stigma? Let's look at five tips from the experts:

1. *Disclose it up front.* If you decide to disclose the stigma to potential buyers, experts agree that it is best to tell them as quickly as possible. By doing so, you can begin to overcome the stigma by selling the home's features. If a buyer learns of the stigma after he has made an offer, he may want to renegotiate or back out of the sale at the last minute.

In New Mexico, a couple who paid more than full price for a home that had been the site of a rape and murder a few days before Halloween 2005 were told up front about the home's history. "It was just a horrible thing that happened. . . . But we don't think of it. It doesn't affect us."

2. *Consider a price adjustment.* Attempting to secure top dollar for a home that was the site of a recent violent crime is probably a losing proposition, especially if you need to sell quickly. To establish value, many successful sellers conduct a preappraisal. This can help to establish an "unimpaired value" for a home, while taking into account homes that have sold with a similar stigma.

3. *Calm their fears.* Homes that have been stigmatized by more down-to-earth issues like "acts of God," including fires, floods, hurricanes, or even tornadoes, may be easier to sell if a buyer's fears can be calmed. For instance, Michael Hall, a state-certified real estate appraiser in Waco, Texas, advised the sellers of a home that had been the site of a devastating fire to provide buyers with:

- A report from the fire department, insurance company, or other experts that explained the cause of the fire.
- A detailed summary of the restoration, including replacement of all walls, sheetrock, joists, rafters, trusses, wiring, fixtures, finishes, and electrical and mechanical systems.
- A written report from a real estate inspector or engineer on the current state of the home.

4. *Remodel the home.* Many homeowners who are forced to deal with a stigma find it wise to remodel the area of the home where the event occurred. By removing all traces of the event from the home, sellers can reduce a buyer's natural tendency to let her imagination run wild. For instance, an agent might explain, "I'm sure you are aware of the home's history. But I can tell you that the home has since been completely remodeled. Every room has been completely renovated."

5. *Be patient.* When an event like a murder or a suicide is fresh in the mind of a community, it can cause buyers to question whether they want to be associated with the tragedy. In addition, some buyers may also be leery of being seen as opportunistic or just plain weird for buying a home that has a stigma. However, time can often cause these concerns to diminish and even disappear.

A good example of the virtues of being patient is the condo on Bundy Drive, which sold for a heavily discounted $590,000, but is now on the market at a whopping $1.8 million! In a report to ABC News, Denise Brown concludes, "I guess real estate wise, I mean thinking now, oh my gosh the property's worth so much we probably should have hung on to it."

By dealing with a stigma head on, many sellers have been able to turn a tragedy into a triumph. But one obstacle may still remain because, amazingly, one of the biggest reasons why a home can sit listlessly on the market has nothing to do with the home itself, but everything to do with you, the homeowner. You, my friend, might just be the problem.

Three Reasons to Fire Yourself

"Okay, big shot, are you ready for the truth?" One of my good friends was looking at a home I had recently purchased as an investment and was now ready to place back on the market.

"I know you love this house, but you're never going to sell it at this price."

What! I was furious. Who did he think he was, telling me that I couldn't get top dollar for my investment? I had run the comparables, and I had even taken the time to visit each home. The home was so priced competitively!

"Jim, you have only one bath in this house, plus you have to go through the garage to get to the patio." I didn't want to hear it. But he kept telling me anyway. "You don't even have central air in this place, plus the backyard needs to be completely torn out." I felt like plugging my ears, but like a jackhammer he kept hammering away. "You need a new garage door, and the front door needs to be painted."

He was right, of course, but it was a hard dose of truth to swallow. As a seller, especially a private seller attempting to sell on your own, it's tempting to think that you will be as effective as an outsider in marketing your own home. But this is often not the case. Why? We tend to overprice our homes, gloss over condition problems, and, worst of all, fail to sell the home effectively to buyers during showings.

This is exactly why if your home seems to be stagnating, with no showings or offers, it might be high time to consider firing yourself. I know this might seem drastic, but removing your ego from the equation, ask yourself: *What was it that motivated you to consider selling the home on your own in the first place?* For most sellers, the answer has two key parts: you wanted to save the real estate fee, and/or you felt you could do a better job than a real estate professional.

Let's look at the last issue first: Can you do a better job than a real estate professional? If the home hasn't sold in the first four to six weeks, you are now facing the law of diminishing returns. This means that even if you continue to pour money into marketing, the reality is that all of the available buyers who are willing to look at For Sale by Owners will have already reviewed your home and rejected it. Your only hope now is to capture the small percentage of new buyers entering the market who are willing to view For Sale by Owner properties. By not listing with an agent, you are missing out on the vast majority of buyers who prefer to view homes with the aid of a real estate professional.

I know—*but what about the commission?* As a real estate professional, I'll admit that I'm biased, but here's the way I see this issue. The fact is, most sellers will end up either paying a fee to a real estate agent or providing a commensurate price adjustment to a buyer in exchange for his buying a home For Sale by Owner. Come on, most buyers aren't going to go through the hassle of driving themselves around, arranging their own financing, negotiating directly with a seller, and then closing their own sale for free. They're going to want something in return, namely, a commission. In fact, many buyers will bluntly say something like, "Listen, because there are no real estate agents involved, would you agree to discount your price by X percent?" Watch out! As soon as you agree to this, you have paid a real estate fee, but you get to do all the work that an agent would have done on your behalf.

> **STRATEGY 58**
>
> Decide in advance when you will fire yourself.

Sure, many sellers can and do sell their homes by owner, and some of them do save money on commissions, but in this appendix we're talking about homes that aren't selling, homes that are stagnating. At some point, many sellers may need to pull the trigger and make the hard decision that as much as they don't want to do it, it's time to fire themselves and hire a real estate professional.

To decide if it's time for you to call in a hired gun, let's look at the three biggest reasons to fire yourself:

1. *No showings.* Your home can't sell unless it's shown to buyers. While your first instinct might be to reduce the price, the truth is that if it is a For Sale by Owner, this may not help. Instead, the problem may be that the home is simply not being exposed to enough of the market. By listing the home, you will instantly tap into the vast majority of buyers who prefer to work only with a real estate professional.

2. *No offers.* Selling a home isn't as easy as it looks on TV. Even for sellers who find themselves knee deep in buyer showings, converting these tire kickers into qualified buyers can be a challenge. Why? Buyers are often uncomfortable dealing with a seller directly; this is one of the reasons that they prefer to work with a third-party buffer like a real estate agent.

3. *No interest.* Selling a home is a full-time job. This is why, for sellers who already have a full-time job, the fun and excitement of trying to market a home can quickly fade. Like a pilot who nods off after flying for hours, this can be a dangerous position to find yourself in. Instead, successful sellers who find themselves growing weary of the sales process wisely turn over the reins to a real estate professional.

So have you failed if you can't sell your home on your own? Absolutely not! Remember, nearly 85 percent of all sellers end up working with a real estate professional. Why? For the same reason that you don't often see surgeons working on themselves or attorneys representing themselves. They know the value of hiring an expert, someone who can help them accomplish their goals, offer sound advice, and provide unemotional counsel.

Index

226

Index